THE JUBILEE PRINCIPLE

THE JUBILEE PRINCIPLE

GOD'S PLAN FOR ECONOMIC FREEDOM

By Dan L. White

WND BOOKS

THE JUBILEE PRINCIPLE
A WND Books book
Published by WorldNetDaily
Los Angeles, CA
Copyright © 2009 by Dan L. White

Jacket design by Genesis Group

WND Books are distributed to the trade by:
Midpoint Trade Books
27 West 20th Street, Suite 1102
New York, NY 10011

WND Books are available at special discounts for bulk purchases. WND Books, Inc. also publishes books in electronic formats. For more information call (310) 961-4170 or visit www.wndbooks.com.

ISBN 13-Digit: 9781935071112
ISBN 10-Digit: 1935071114
E-Book ISBN 13-Digit: 9781935071655
E-Book ISBN 10-Digit: 1-935071653
Library of Congress Control Number: 2009931565

Printed in the United States of America

10 9 8 7 6 5 4 3 2 1

TABLE OF CONTENTS

This book talks about economic depressions and the economic long wave, but it is not a book about finance. It is a book about God and His people. There is a striking correlation between the long wave in free economies and the design of the Hebrews' economy as set up by God for Israel. This book is an intensive study of how Yahweh, the God of the Bible, set Israel up economically. It is based on the premises that the God of the Bible is the Creator of everything, that His spiritual law is fully in force, and that the Bible is His divine instruction. It discusses how much time God expects His people to spend with Him, and how that will affect an individual.

It is expected that most people who are interested in this discussion will be intimately familiar with the Bible and will be eager for such an in-depth examination. It may well be that some who are less familiar with the Bible will also be interested in this discussion, because of the interesting parallels between God's spiritual law and the consistent economic pattern seen over the centuries.

CHAPTER 1

NIKOLAI AND MOSES

People act in generally predictable ways, but always with individual variations.

Today I am going to eat lunch. Right now, though, I don't know what I am going to have for lunch. Tuna or turkey?

We can predict that humans will always fight wars. We cannot predict who will be involved or exactly when the wars will occur. Those are individual variations. But based on the history of the human race, we can say that humans will fight wars.

Human nature does not change, and consistent reactions to similar conditions create cycles that repeat. The specifics of these cycles vary, but the overall cycle recurs, including the boom-bust economic cycle that "busted" in 2008. Human nature repeats, so the cycle repeats. Everyone knows about the Great Depression of the 1930s. Few know that it was just one in a recurring series of economic busts which followed economic booms.

One economist grew famous for having studied the boom-bust cycle. Russian Nikolai Kondratieff developed the first Russian five-year plan soon after the 1917 Bolshevik Revolution to try to assist the fledgling communist government.

He also undertook an economic study to try to find factors that would help the economic growth of the new post-tsar Russia. What that communist official found was a long-term economic cycle in capitalism. He published this in a 1926 report, "Long Waves in Economic Life."[1]

Kondratieff studied the period from 1789 to 1926 in American, British, and French economies, observing prices and interest rates. He believed that capitalist economies showed a long wave boom-bust cycle of about fifty to sixty years. The bust cycle was a correction of boom excesses.[2] "He saw the capitalist world economy as evolving and self-correcting and, by implication, he denied the notion of an approaching collapse of capitalism then current among Marxist economists."[3]

Communism claimed that capitalism would self-destruct. Therefore, Kondratieff's view that capitalism corrected itself was an implied criticism of the communist movement. He set out to help the new government and wound up its enemy.

Joseph Stalin wanted to collectivize all Russian agriculture, to make it more productive than it supposedly would be under private ownership. Comrade K's conclusion that capitalism did not self-destruct but self-corrected directly contradicted Comrade Stalin's policy. In 1928 Kondratieff lost his job as director of the Institute for the Study of Business Activity. In 1930 he was imprisoned in the Russian Gulag. In 1938 he was sentenced to death.[4]

Although the communists didn't appreciate Kondratieff's work, others—on the capitalist side—did notice it. Shortly after Kondratieff made his boom-bust cycle observations, the capitalist economies went from boom to bust, which seemed to confirm his conclusions. Since that time, the long wave, called the Kondratieff Wave, has gained wide publicity and has undergone further study. For example, Harvard economists studied British wheat prices all the way back to the 1200s and found a long wave cycle averaging fifty-four years.[5]

Financial advisor Dr. Joseph de Beauchamp further explains the long wave:

> [W]hat the Kondratieff Wave is about is a study of long cycles of debt buildup and repudiation. It is not exclusively about price inflation and deflation periods. Deflation is caused in part by the debt collapse. It is also a generational thing as the next cycle of debt buildup and collapse is

renewed every two to three generations as the previous generation that went through comparable periods dies off. The old adage that "this time it is different" means the circumstances are different, yes, but they fail to recognize that the previous period was the same in terms of excesses and therefore the end result is the same.[6]

Notice the premise that the long wave is a cycle of debt buildup and repudiation. The debt builds up during the period of prosperity, not during the period of depression.

That seems backward, doesn't it?

One would expect debt to build up in a period of less wealth, when consumers have less money to use for living expenses, and therefore accumulate debt. To the contrary, debt grows when there is plenty of money and the debt is least needed for normal living expenses.

As of this writing, in 2009, the United States faces a severe financial crisis. Some of the nation's largest banks, brokerages, and insurance firms have been brought to their knees. The government has stepped in with massive bailouts of such scope that it then brings into question the integrity of the whole U.S. financial system, including the United States Treasury.

Joseph Farah of WorldNetDaily wrote in an October 2008 article titled "Forgive Us Our Debts":

> [Y]ou've got to understand the fundamental problem we have is one of gargantuan debt. That's the central problem in the mortgage scandal. It's the reason banks and investment houses are going out of business. It's the reason the stock market is failing. And it's the reason so many Americans, burdened by excessive credit card debt, are hurting.[7]

Financial analyst and writer David Chapman elaborates on the same theme:

> Following the steep secondary recession of the early 1980s the markets embarked into the autumn K-Wave plateau. We had stock market and real estate bubbles, a collapse in

commodity prices, a collapse in interest rates, and low inflation. But we also had a huge buildup in debt that allowed us to buy our way out of the recessions of the early 1980s and early 1990s. Each succeeding recession required higher levels of debt to purchase an additional dollar of GDP.

Now the debt has become unsustainable and the ability to buy our way out of further problems is severely compromised. One only needs to look at the decade-long nightmare of Japan to see that zero interest rates and all the stimulation in the world has failed to bring it out of its slump. We are witnessing merely the beginning of the debt implosion that inevitably follows the excesses.[8]

The *Wall Street Journal* chimed in:

The U.S. financial system resembles a patient in intensive care. The body is trying to fight off a disease that is spreading, and as it does so, the body convulses, settles for a time, and then convulses again. The illness seems to be overwhelming the self-healing tendencies of markets.

Fed and Treasury officials have identified the disease. It's called deleveraging, or the unwinding of debt. During the credit boom, financial institutions and American households took on too much debt. Between 2002 and 2006, household borrowing grew at an average annual rate of 11 percent, far outpacing overall economic growth. Borrowing by financial institutions grew by a 10 percent annualized rate. Now many of those borrowers can't pay back the loans, a problem that is exacerbated by the collapse in housing prices. They need to reduce their dependence on borrowed money, a painful and drawn-out process that can choke off credit and economic growth.[9]

The *Wall Street Journal* article points out some examples of accumulating debt, not out of need, but out of greed:

Hedge funds could be among the next problem areas. Many rely on borrowed money to amplify their returns. With banks under pressure, many hedge funds are less able to borrow this money now, pressuring returns. Meanwhile, there are growing indications that fewer investors are shifting into hedge funds while others are pulling out. Fund investors are dealing with their own problems: Many have taken out loans to make their investments and are finding it more difficult now to borrow.[10]

Aggressive investors borrowed money to multiply returns. They were not just trying to get a good investment return on their capital. They were trying to get a good investment return on others' capital, too.

The core of this financial crisis was not the stock market or even Wall Street. The core of this financial crisis was the housing market. Not so much commercial real estate, but Mom and Pop and Uncle Jim real estate—just plain housing that just plain people buy.

Then Secretary of the Treasury Henry Paulson said, "The root of the problem lies in this housing correction."[11]

All of Wall Street has been turned upside down by Main Street!

Paulson continued by saying that until "the biggest part of that is behind us and we have more stability in housing prices, we are going to continue to have turmoil in the financial markets."[12]

Financial writer Laura Rowley made the following comments:

> The root of the problem is a cocktail of debt with a chaser of pathological optimism, and many Americans got drunk on both. Awash in credit offers, they bought homes, cars, and lots of other stuff they couldn't afford, and hoped for a best-case scenario, in which their home values and rising salaries would take care of it.
>
> There were plenty of foolish, crooked, and greedy intermediaries who played key roles in the meltdown—from the Federal Reserve, which held interest rates too low for too long; to mortgage brokers who defrauded borrowers; to the investment houses that securitized and sold toxic mortgage derivatives.[13]

Again, notice that the debt did not grow during a period of depression or great need. Consumers built the debt up during a period of great prosperity and great greed.

Alan Greenspan, former head of the Fed, said that the United States is in a once-in-a-century financial crisis. This is the worst economy he's ever seen.[14]

If we go back a century, that takes us to the Panic of 1907.

The Great Depression that began in 1929 we know about; "Black Tuesday" of 1987 most of us remember; but have you heard of the Panic of 1907? An article from the Federal Reserve Archival System for Economic Research discusses that panic, which actually led to the creation of the Federal Reserve System:

> For the past two centuries recurrent crises have shaken the banking system and financial markets in the United States. One severe crisis, the Bank Panic of 1907, disrupted financial markets to such an extent that it became an important catalyst for creating the Federal Reserve and the U.S. Banking system as it operates today.
>
> The panic was precipitated by a shady financial scheme by wealthy people to increase their wealth.
>
> Any shock to the financial markets could, and in 1907 did, spark a major crisis. Such a shock occurred on October 16, 1907, when F. Augustus Heinze's attempt to corner the stock of United Copper Company failed. Although United Copper was only modestly significant, the collapse of Heinze's scheme, which came atop a slowing economy, a declining stock market, and a tight money market, sparked one of the most severe bank panics of the National Banking Era...
>
> As Heinze's extensive involvement in banking became apparent, along with that of another speculator associated with the copper scam, C. F. Morse, depositors' fears of insolvency precipitated a series of runs on the banks where the two men held prominent positions.[15]

What caused that problem? Greed. Some tried to corner the market in a copper company; people had gone into debt by borrowing money from banks to multiply their profits.

As a result of that episode, the Federal Reserve Bank was formed, to keep such a thing from happening again. And yet multiple giant financial institutions have fallen, in spite of the Federal Reserve's extreme efforts. Presently the Fed is trying to save not just an institution here and there, but the whole U.S. financial system.

How did this happen?

Greed and debt.

Because of greed, people and institutions took on more and more debt. Finally the pyramid collapsed.

In the essay "The Great Depression: Can It Happen Again?" John Wallis discusses the leverage stock traders had in 1929:

> In 1929 stock could be bought on as low as a 10 percent margin: a $10 stock could be bought with a $1 investment and a $9 loan. The minimum margin rate is regulated today at 50 percent; the same $10 stock requires an investment of $5 and a $5 loan. Since the stock itself is collateral for the loan, when the price of the stock falls the lender, usually a broker, calls in part of the loan. If a $10 stock drops by $1, the investor with a 10 percent margin must come up with another dollar—a loss of 100 percent on the investment. The investor with a 50 percent margin must come up with the same dollar, but loses only 20 percent. If a margin call is not met, the broker sells the stock to cover the investor's loan. In severe market downturns, declining stock prices snowball as margin calls are made and investors sell their stock to meet their calls.[16]

That was paying for prosperity on credit, or debt. When someone bought stock in a company for 10 percent down, that meant he had a debt of 90 percent. That also meant that nine times more money paid for the stock than was actually available. Naturally that drove the prices higher.

Most investors then fell into the trap of thinking that stock prices could not fall. When they did reach unsustainable levels and began to fall, the brokers called for the stock traders to put up more money over and above the original 10 percent. Often the speculators were so heavily margined that they couldn't come up with extra funds, because they had invested so heavily to make as much money as possible on the "sure-thing market." Then the brokers had to sell those stocks. That drove down the prices of those stocks, which caused still more margin calls, which caused the brokers to have to sell more, which drove down the prices still more.

On and on it went until disaster struck.

The same thing has now happened in real estate, except worse.

First of all, there was the absurd idea that real estate prices always go up. *"They're not making any more land, you know."*

People were buying real estate with nothing down. Remember: in the 1920s people bought stocks with 10 percent down and 90 percent debt. In the recent real estate boom, people bought real estate with *nothing down and 100 percent debt.* Sometimes people had loans where they didn't even have to make the normal monthly interest payments, so that the buyer actually fell further in debt with every passing month. Everyone thought that the difference would be made up in a few years when the buyer sold the real estate—at a higher price, of course.

Furthermore, people who bought real estate with 100 percent leverage often lied about their ability to pay for it. Banks often required no documented proof of income.

This extreme use of debt drove up the price of real estate far beyond its normal economic value. Home prices soared about 85 percent from 1996 through 2006 in inflation-adjusted dollars.

Consider that fact. Not only did we have inflation and the lessening value of the dollar pushing home prices up, but housing prices nearly doubled in a decade—even after accounting for inflation.

I live in the Ozarks where the land is pretty, but not very productive. Laura Ingalls Wilder, who wrote the *Little House* books, moved here with her husband Almanzo in 1894. When they first saw the country, Almanzo said it was so pretty that they might be able to live just from the looks of it.[17] But they couldn't, of course. They raised chickens and cows, planted apple trees, and lived from that. The recent rise in land prices, though, means that the land here will not pay for itself in cows or hay, which it ultimately has to do, unless you are just going to live "off the looks of it."

The recent housing boom was living room speculation; literally speculating, not on Wall Street stocks, but on living rooms and kitchens and two and a half baths. The same mentality which applied to stocks in 1929 applied to houses in 2006. *The price can't go down. Buy houses on total margin, with nothing down. Stretch your financial qualifications to get more loans to make more money as real estate appreciates. Buy a house, keep it for a few years, or a year, or perhaps even a week or two, and profit handsomely.*

There is even a term for Main Street housing speculation— *flipping.* Buy a house and put it back on the market immediately for more than you paid. Flip it. Some people were professional flippers.

Finally, this pyramid scheme had to falter. It got flipped upside down.

Some people, those who could least afford their aggressive mortgages, could not keep up with their payments. Just like the brokers making a margin call, the banks foreclosed on some properties. Those properties then went on the market, forcing prices down and hurting new construction and other related earnings, which gave many people still less money to make payments. That caused more foreclosures, which put more properties on the market, which drove down prices still further.

This mountain of debt was caused by greed. Americans were not just looking for a place to live—they were looking to live it up. The average size of a new house went up by about six hundred square feet in the last few years, while the average number of people living in a home decreased.[18] A number of Americans bought second homes or vacation homes or condos. Do people really need multiple homes? *Well, not only could they use them part time, but they were a good investment, you know.*

9

Greed and debt.

Now the United States is in its worst financial crisis at least since the Great Depression, or perhaps the Panic of 1907, or maybe ever. It does not seem likely that the effects of this will stop with the demise of financial institutions. Surely the panic that began with speculating on Main Street living rooms will wind up in Main Street kitchens.

And it seems that Nikolai Kondratieff's long wave has appeared again. That cycle which has been traced back to the 1200s seems to have recurred in the 2000s. That cycle is based in human nature. Because of greed, not need, humans build up debt. Them that dance must pay the fiddler. About every fifty years or so, the fiddler gets paid, and the debt gets worked off.

The economic long wave is a naturally occurring cycle. When people have the freedom to run their own financial affairs, they ride the boom-bust roller coaster up and down about twice a century, as if a natural law is operating. Ultimately, though, the cause of the boom-bust cycle is not money, but the human nature of those who pursue money. That natural law, then, must be a law about human nature.

In the Bible, the Jubilee cycle also occurred about twice a century. That cycle was set up by the God of the Bible, who has much to say about human nature and natural law.

CHAPTER 2

NATURAL LAW

W*hen you think about it*, if a cycle in prices and interest rates has been observed from the thirteenth century through the twenty-first century, what does that mean?

It means there has to be in place a functioning law.

If I throw a ball up, and sometimes it comes back down, and sometimes it stays up in the air, I can't tell much from that. That's a hit-or-miss proposition. The ball might come back. Then again it might not.

If I throw the ball up ten times, and ten times that ball comes back down, then I'm on to something. There is law operating there.

Natural law rules in everything that we know and observe.

What a phenomenal statement that is. Everything that we know and see operates according to law.

Take the universe. Moons circle planets, planets orbit stars, stars whoosh through their galaxies, and galaxies gallop through the universe, all with lawful precision and predictability.

At the other extreme, if we compare the endless enormity of space with the microscopic composition of an atom, we again find the same punctilious predictability. Electrons, protons, neutrons, and quarks all operate according to certain operative principles. Quarks are not quirky. Actually, they behave meekly, according to law.

The ecology of our beloved blue planet functions according to natural law. If we go against that law, our ecology and our lives suffer. We are continually learning how delicate Earth's ecosystems are and what havoc we wreak when we disregard them. If we pollute California, we make smog, and our eyes burn and we can't see Mount Wilson from the palmed streets of Pasadena. When the Chinese have two cars in every garage as Americans have, we may not be able to see the moon. Without dipping into the charade of "global warming," much of the earth has been polluted, with dirty rivers and lakes, and even trashed oceans and skies. To the degree that we do that, we all suffer, because of natural law.

As we zoom in from the whole world to your backyard, we still deal with natural law. You may plant a garden, hoping for a hundred-fold return of the seeds you bury. This return will be controlled by established principles which neither you nor I nor any human set in motion. Your backyard garden depends on how well you and your environment operate within those principles. If you obey the precepts of agronomy, you will multiply the seed. If you don't, you will waste your labor and resources. The natural law will prevail.

Is it not perfectly logical, then, that natural law also applies to human conduct, just as it does to everything else in existence?

Are you fat? A couch potato? A smoker? Those choices will affect you. If you want to stay healthy, then you must try to live by certain principles of health. You may not like going hungry, or exercising, or giving up smoking, but to enjoy maximum health, you must do those things, like it or not. You cannot change the natural law. You can only decide how much you will try to live within that law. You can't make the law. You only decide if you will break the law.

The mental and spiritual processes of humans are just as subject to natural law as everything else.

Did I make a big jump in logic there?

When I said that the spiritual activities of humans are just as subject to natural law as everything else, I just went from smoking to smirking, from eating to meditating, and from sitting on your couch to serving others.

Is that not also eminently sensible? Would human mental processes be the only thing in existence not subject to natural law?

Surely not.

John Robbins, of the Baskin-Robbins ice cream chain, said this in his book *Healthy at 100*:

> Thirty years ago, anyone who said there were profound medical consequences to human relationships would have had their sanity questioned by modern science. And anyone blaming loneliness for physical illness would have been laughed at. But in the last few decades there has been an explosion of scientific understanding about the deep connections between interpersonal relationships and health.
>
> As you may know, there is in Western medicine a great deal of concern about risk factors like high blood pressure, high cholesterol, smoking, and obesity—and deservedly so, for they are very often linked to serious disease. But an ever-increasing body of medical research is coming to the surprising conclusion that the quality of your relationships with other people is every bit as important to your health as these indicators—if not more so. Chronic loneliness now ranks as one of the most lethal risk factors determining who will die prematurely in modern industrialized nations.[1]

Love makes longevity.

Health magazines tout not only diet and exercise, but the importance of your circle of friends to your health. Statistically, the person who can expect the shortest lifespan is the unmarried person. A correlation has even been found between a heart attack victim's recovery rate and whether or not the victim has a pet.

Sharing affection with family, friends, or even a pet is in harmony with natural law and has a positive effect on people.

Again, the mental or spiritual activities of humans are just as subject to natural law as everything physical is. A society is a family grown very large. Therefore, the same natural law that governs an individual and a family would also apply to society.

So what is the natural law ruling in the actions of people?

Albert Einstein calculated the equation telling how much energy is in mass: $e=mc^2$. That led to the atomic bomb. Then he spent the rest of his life trying to find a unified force theory to explain the four fundamental forces—strong nuclear, weak nuclear, electromagnetic, and gravity—in terms of a single unified force. He never found it. No one has.

And here I am, ready to reveal to you the force which rules in the affairs of people.

I will state unequivocally, then, that the basis of all natural law and all forces in creation is God:

> This is what Yahweh, the King of Israel, and his Redeemer, Yahweh of Armies, says: "I am the first, and I am the last; and besides me there is no God. Who is like me? Who will call, and will declare it, and set it in order for me, since I established the ancient people? Let them declare the things that are coming, and that will happen. Don't fear, neither be afraid. Haven't I declared it to you long ago, and shown it? You are my witnesses. Is there a God besides me? Indeed, there is not. I don't know any other Rock" (Isaiah 44:6-8).[1]

> I am Yahweh, and there is none else. Besides me, there is no God. I will strengthen you, though you have not known me; that they may know from the rising of the sun, and from the west, that there is none besides me. I am Yahweh, and there is no one else. I form the light, and create darkness. I make peace, and create calamity. I am Yahweh, who does all these things. Distil, you heavens, from above, and let the skies pour down righteousness. Let the earth open, that it may bring forth salvation, and let it cause righteousness to spring up with it. I, Yahweh, have created it (Isaiah 45:5-8).

> Declare and present it. Yes, let them take counsel together. Who has shown this from ancient time? Who has declared it of old? Haven't I, Yahweh? There is no other God besides me, a just God and a Savior; There is no one besides me.

---

[1] All Bible quotes, unless otherwise noted, are from the *World English Bible*, which is based on the American Standard Version.

> Look to me, and be saved, all the ends of the earth; for I am God, and there is no other. By myself have I sworn, the word has gone forth from my mouth in righteousness, and will not return, that to me every knee shall bow, every tongue shall swear. They will say of me, "There is righteousness and strength only in Yahweh." Even to him shall men come; and all those who were incensed against him shall be disappointed (Isaiah 45:21-24).

God's personal name in the third commandment and in about seven thousand references in the Hebrew Scriptures is *Yahweh*. That name simply means "to be."

He is.

Without Him, nothing else is.

Law requires a force to uphold it. That force behind all law is Yahweh God. And the natural law governing all human conduct is this:

> Master, which is the great commandment in the law? Jesus said unto him, Thou shalt love the Lord thy God with all thy heart, and with all thy soul, and with all thy mind. This is the first and great commandment. And the second is like unto it, Thou shalt love thy neighbour as thyself. On these two commandments hang all the law and the prophets (Matthew 22:36-40, KJV).

I repeat: the natural law governing all human conduct is this, now in a modern translation.

> Teacher, what is the most important commandment in the Law? Jesus answered: Love the Lord your God with all your heart, soul, and mind. This is the first and most important commandment. The second most important commandment is like this one. And it is, Love others as much as you love yourself. All the Law of Moses and the Books of the Prophets are based on these two commandments (Matthew 22:36-40, CEV).

The natural law is to love God with all your heart and to love your neighbor as yourself.

The Messiah Jesus, or, more accurately, Y'shua, was not making this up on the spur of the moment. The two great commandments were not a new teaching. Indeed, He was quoting the *Torah*, the first five books of the Old Testament, *the Law*. The Hebrew Names Version of Matthew makes that a little clearer.

> "Rabbi, which is the greatest *mitzvah* in the *Torah*?" Yeshua said to him, "'You shall love the Lord your God with all your heart, with all your soul, and with all your mind.' This is the first and great *mitzvah*. A second likewise is this, 'You shall love your neighbor as yourself.' The whole *Torah* and the Prophets depend on these two *mitzvot*" (Matthew 22: 36-40).

The *Torah* is the collection of the first five books of the Bible, called the Book of the Law. Apparently Moses wrote those down, covering the period from Creation to the Exodus and the wanderings in the wilderness. That which Jesus or Y'shua cited as the two great commandments were from these old books.

Here's the first great commandment:

> Hear, Israel: Yahweh is our God; Yahweh is one: and you shall love Yahweh your God with all your heart, and with all your soul, and with all your might (Deuteronomy 6:4-5).

> Now, Israel, what does Yahweh your God require of you, but to fear Yahweh your God, to walk in all his ways, and to love him, and to serve Yahweh your God with all your heart and with all your soul, to keep the commandments of Yahweh, and his statutes, which I command you this day for your good? (Deuteronomy 10:12-3).

> Yahweh your God will circumcise your heart, and the heart of your seed, to love Yahweh your God with all your heart, and with all your soul, that you may live (Deuteronomy 30:6).

And the second great commandment:

> You shall not hate your brother in your heart. You shall surely rebuke your neighbor, and not bear sin because of him. You shall not take vengeance, nor bear any grudge

against the children of your people; but you shall love your neighbor as yourself. I am Yahweh (Leviticus 19:17-18).

Here is an example, from the *Torah*, of putting the second great commandment into action:

If you meet your enemy's ox or his donkey going astray, you shall surely bring it back to him again. If you see the donkey of him who hates you fallen down under his burden, don't leave him, you shall surely help him with it (Exodus 23:4-5).

This is the natural law applied—deliver your enemy's donkey. Of course your human nature would lead you to hit your enemy's donkey when he's down. But if you are intent on hitting a donkey, then you will break the natural law to love your neighbor as yourself. Not only will you hurt your neighbor, you will hurt yourself. And you will hurt the donkey, of course.

Do you remember the story of Cain and Abel? They were the first two children born on Earth. Cain asked the burning question which echoes all down through human history:

The man knew Eve his wife. She conceived, and gave birth to Cain, and said, "I have gotten a man with Yahweh's help." Again she gave birth, to Cain's brother Abel. Abel was a keeper of sheep, but Cain was a tiller of the ground. As time passed, it happened that Cain brought an offering to Yahweh from the fruit of the ground. Abel also brought some of the firstborn of his flock and of its fat. Yahweh respected Abel and his offering, but he didn't respect Cain and his offering. Cain was very angry, and the expression on his face fell. Yahweh said to Cain, "Why are you angry? Why has the expression of your face fallen? If you do well, will it not be lifted up? If you don't do well, sin crouches at the door. Its desire is for you, but you are to rule over it." Cain said to Abel, his brother, "Let's go into the field." It happened when they were in the field that Cain rose up against Abel, his brother, and killed him. Yahweh said to Cain, "Where is Abel, your brother?" He said, "I don't know. Am I my brother's keeper?" (Genesis 4:1-9).

Am I my brother's keeper? It is taken for granted that I am the keeper of me. Should I also keep him, just the same as I keep me? That is the law. Love your neighbor as yourself. You are your neighbor's keeper. "Do to others as you would have them do to you" (Luke 6:31, BBE).

The Ten Commandments, taught to Israel at the time of the Exodus from Egypt, provided detailed explanations of these two broad principles. But they did not take effect then. Shortly after Creation, when Cain killed Abel, that was sin, which broke the Ten Commandments already in effect. At Mount Sinai, Israel was retaught those commandments with a personal visit from Yahweh God Himself.

The first four commandments explain how to love Yahweh, and the last six explain how to love your neighbor as yourself. For example, if you love your father and mother, you will honor them. If you love your neighbor, you won't kill him. If you love your neighbor, you also won't steal his wife, steal his goods, lie to him, or even want to take what is his.

In the New Testament, Paul understood the basis of God's law when he wrote, "For all the law is made complete in one word, even in this, Have love for your neighbor as for yourself" (Galatians 5:14, BBE).

Likewise James, Christ's brother, agreed.

> But if you keep the greatest law of all, as it is given in the holy writings, Have love for your neighbor as for yourself, you do well: But if you take a man's position into account, you do evil, and are judged as evildoers by the law. For anyone who keeps all the law, but makes a slip in one point, is judged to have gone against it all. For he who said, Do not be untrue in married life, is the same who said, Put no man to death. Now if you are not untrue in married life, but you put a man to death, the law is broken. Let your words and your acts be those of men who are to be judged by the law which makes free (James 2:8-12, BBE).

Cain asked the question, *Am I my brother's keeper?* He did not think he was. Cain's sacrifice did not please Yahweh, while his brother's did. Therefore Abel became Cain's competition. Abel's sacrifice had been accepted, so Cain made a sacrifice out of Abel.

Cain simply looked out for himself. He loved himself more than anyone. He felt that he had to do that. That's human nature. If he didn't look out for himself, who would look out for him?

These Ten Commandments, direct from the finger of the Creator and the mount of the Messiah, underpin everything in creation—from your interactions with your family and neighbors to the economy. *Love God with all your heart, and love your neighbor as yourself.*

CHAPTER 3

WHOLLY HOLY WRIT

W*hen Yahweh put Israel in Israel*, he wasn't just improvising. He had a plan. They were a special people in a special place, and God gave them special teaching. Fortunately, we have a copy, the Hebrew Scriptures.

Most Christians slight the Hebrew Scriptures, which they call the Old Testament (which, incidentally, makes up most of the Bible).

Gideons are now forbidden from handing out Bibles in America's public schools. They are reduced to handing out the Scriptures in Christian schools and at Christian homeschool gatherings. Often, they will hand out to young people a small New Testament, tucked easily into a pocket and carried around with the student. Indeed, it takes a young person to read one of these New Testaments, because the print is far too small for older eyes.

You have often seen these New Testaments. You may have one yourself.

Think about this—have you ever seen a Christian carry an Old Testament?

Jews may carry just the Old Testament, because they do not accept the New Testament. Christians accept the Hebrew Scriptures as part of the inspired word of God, but you have never seen a Christian pass out only an Old Testament, have you?

It's either the whole Bible, or the New Testament, but not just the Old Testament. That shows the relative value that

Christians put on that which makes up about three-fourths of the Bible.

How did the earliest New Testament Christians view what is now called the Old Testament?

Christ knew the Hebrew Scriptures, and helped the disciples understand them:

> Some men from our group went to the tomb and found it just as the women had said. But they didn't see Jesus either. Then Jesus asked the two disciples, "Why can't you understand? How can you be so slow to believe all that the prophets said? Didn't you know that the Messiah would have to suffer before he was given his glory?" Jesus then explained everything written about himself in the Scriptures, beginning with the Law of Moses and the Books of the Prophets (Luke 24:24-27, CEV).

> After Jesus said this, he showed them his hands and his feet. The disciples were so glad and amazed that they could not believe it. Jesus then asked them, "Do you have something to eat?" They gave him a piece of baked fish. He took it and ate it as they watched. Jesus said to them, "While I was still with you, I told you that everything written about me in the Law of Moses, the Books of the Prophets, and in the Psalms had to happen." Then he helped them understand the Scriptures (Luke 24:40-45, CEV).

When Paul taught, he used the Hebrew Scriptures:

> So as usual, Paul went there to worship, and on three Sabbaths he spoke to the people. He used the Scriptures to show them that the Messiah had to suffer, but that he would rise from death. Paul also told them that Jesus is the Messiah he was preaching about (Acts 17:2-3, CEV).

> [A]nd how from childhood you have been acquainted with the sacred writings, which are able to make you wise for salvation through faith in Christ Jesus. All Scripture is breathed out by God and profitable for teaching, for reproof, for correction, and for training in righteousness, that the man of God may be competent, equipped for every good work (2 Timothy 3:15-17, ESV).

Paul told Timothy that everything in the Scriptures is God's Word. Exactly what Scriptures was Paul referring to? The Hebrew Scriptures. The New Testament had not been collected together at that time.

> All of this makes us even more certain that what the prophets said is true. So you should pay close attention to their message, as you would to a lamp shining in some dark place. You must keep on paying attention until daylight comes and the morning star rises in your hearts. But you need to realize that no one alone can understand any of the prophecies in the Scriptures. The prophets did not think these things up on their own, but they were guided by the Spirit of God (2 Peter 1:19-21, CEV).

Peter said that those who wrote the Hebrew Scriptures did not do it on their own, but were guided by the spirit of God. Therefore, when God gives instructions in the Old Testament, they are always instructive. They are never to be disdained. Even if certain instructions have been superseded, such as physical sacrifices, they are still instructive.

God brought His chosen people, Israel, the family of Abraham, into the Holy Land. He gave them detailed instructions about how to live. Those instructions began with the Ten Commandments. Remember that the natural law on which everything was based is the two great commandments, to love God more than yourself and to love your neighbor as yourself.

The first four of the Ten Commandments explain how to love God.

> God spoke all these words, saying, "I am Yahweh your God, who brought you out of the land of Egypt, out of the house of bondage.
>
> "You shall have no other gods before me.
>
> "You shall not make for yourselves an idol, nor any image of anything that is in the heavens above, or that is in the earth beneath, or that is in the water under the earth: you shall not bow yourself down to them, nor serve them, for

I, Yahweh your God, am a jealous God, visiting the iniquity of the fathers on the children, on the third and on the fourth generation of those who hate me, and showing loving kindness to thousands of those who love me and keep my commandments.

"You shall not take the name of Yahweh your God in vain, for Yahweh will not hold him guiltless who takes his name in vain.

"Remember the Sabbath day, to keep it holy. You shall labor six days, and do all your work, but the seventh day is a Sabbath to Yahweh your God. You shall not do any work in it, you, nor your son, nor your daughter, your male servant, nor your female servant, nor your livestock, nor your stranger who is within your gates; for in six days Yahweh made heaven and earth, the sea, and all that is in them, and rested the seventh day; therefore Yahweh blessed the Sabbath day, and made it holy" (Exodus 20:1-11).

The last five commandments explain how to love people:

You shall not kill.

You shall not commit adultery.

You shall not steal.

You shall not bear false witness against your neighbor.

You shall not covet your neighbor's house. You shall not covet your neighbor's wife, nor his manservant, nor his maidservant, nor his ox, nor his ass, nor anything that is your neighbor's (Exodus 20:13-17, MKJV).

The Fifth Commandment connected God and people through parents. It is through parents that children are to learn about God. If the family institution breaks down, the knowledge of God is lost. "Honor your father and your mother, that your days may be long in the land which Yahweh your God gives you" (Exodus 20:12).

The two great commandments and the Ten Commandments make twelve commandments. Twelve is the number of government in the Bible, such as the twelve tribes of Israel and the twelve disciples. These twelve commandments are the guide for God's people.

Beyond these most basic commandments were detailed instructions, which were the applications of the Ten Commandments for Israel at that time.

Some of these instructions involved the economics of that time and that people. These economic principles were also based on the two great commandments. Much can be learned about the mind of God by studying these instructions on economics. Throughout these instructions, we keep coming back to Cain's question—*Am I my brother's keeper?*

Cain did not think he was his brother's keeper. He was self-seeking; Cain came first. In reality, giving Cain's answer to Cain's question, or being selfish, is the cause of the Kondratieff Wave. The more people get, the more they want. God's law, on the other hand, is to love God and others. Therefore, His economic system is based on love for God and others more than love of self.

CHAPTER 4

MANNA AND MONEY

How can there be an economic system based on love for God and others?

Adam Smith is known as the father of modern economics and he wrote what is considered the first work of modern economics, *The Wealth of Nations*. In that eighteenth century work, he held that people who pursue their own selfish economic interests ultimately work for the good of the whole society. Each producer self-centeredly searches for the best way to maximize his profits. He would like to sell his product for all he can get. Each consumer self-centeredly searches for the best deal. He would like to pay almost nothing for everything he buys. Yet operating together, the producer sells a product that the consumer can afford at a price that allows the producer to stay in business. An "invisible hand" based on selfishness guides this process. Adam Smith wrote:

> Every individual necessarily labours to render the annual revenue of the society as great as he can. He generally neither intends to promote the public interest, nor knows how much he is promoting it.... He intends only his own gain, and he is in this, as in many other cases, led by an invisible hand to promote an end which was no part of his intention. Nor is it always the worse for society that it was no part of his intention. By pursuing his own interest he frequently promotes that of the society more effectually than when he really intends to promote it. I have never known much good done by those who affected to trade for the public good.[1]

The point there is that self-interest leads to the benefit of all in a free economy. If I am a farmer and I want to sell my crops, it is to my advantage to produce as fine a product as I can, because I get more for it. At the same time, that benefits those who buy my crops, because they get a better product.

Notice this verse:

> But in the latter days, it will happen that the mountain of Yahweh's temple will be established on the top of the mountains, and it will be exalted above the hills; and peoples will stream to it. Many nations will go and say, "Come, and let us go up to the mountain of Yahweh, and to the house of the God of Jacob; and he will teach us of his ways, and we will walk in his paths." For out of Zion will go forth the law, and the word of Yahweh from Jerusalem; and he will judge between many peoples, and will decide concerning strong nations afar off. They will beat their swords into plowshares, and their spears into pruning hooks. Nation will not lift up sword against nation, neither will they learn war any more. But they will sit every man under his vine and under his fig tree; and no one will make them afraid: For the mouth of Yahweh of Armies has spoken (Micah 4:1-4).

In the millennial kingdom pointed to here, every man will sit under his vine and his fig tree. That will not be Joseph Stalin's vine or fig tree. Each person will have his own property to use.

The United States was begun as a socialist experiment. Both in Virginia at Jamestown and in New England at Plymouth Colony, they began with socialist principles. Every man did not have his own vine and fig tree, but they all had everything together.

They nearly starved.

Only when they established the principle that each family ate what they themselves produced did they begin to have enough food.

Since that time, the United States has had one of the least socialistic economies in the world. In the last century, though, the United States has continually trended toward more socialism. One of the key reasons for this is that its school system is socialistic, a tax-supported government monopoly. All public school students learn to accept socialism to some degree, because they are educated in a socialist system. They bring that attitude into the rest of their lives.

When Yahweh brought Israel into the Holy Land, He let each family have their own property to take care of. It was theirs to use in perpetuity—as long as they obeyed Him. That's a type of free economy capitalism.

However, when humans own private property, they also have human nature. That human nature goes to excess.

Look at this example of the manna:

> They took their journey from Elim, and all the congregation of the children of Israel came to the wilderness of Sin, which is between Elim and Sinai, on the fifteenth day of the second month after their departing out of the land of Egypt. The whole congregation of the children of Israel murmured against Moses and against Aaron in the wilderness; and the children of Israel said to them, "We wish that we had died by the hand of Yahweh in the land of Egypt, when we sat by the meat pots, when we ate our fill of bread, for you have brought us out into this wilderness, to kill this whole assembly with hunger" (Exodus 16:1-3).

Israel was hungry. Hunger is hard. Either they could ask God for food, or they could gripe about not having any.

They griped:

> Then said Yahweh to Moses, "Behold, I will rain bread from the sky for you, and the people shall go out and gather a day's portion every day, that I may test them, whether they will walk in my law, or not. It shall come to pass on the sixth day, that they shall prepare that which they bring in, and it shall be twice as much as they gather daily." Moses and Aaron said to all the children of Israel, "At evening, then you shall know that Yahweh has brought you out from the land of Egypt; and in the morning, then you shall see the glory of Yahweh; because he hears your murmurings against Yahweh. Who are we, that you murmur against us?" Moses said, "Now Yahweh

shall give you meat to eat in the evening, and in the morning bread to satisfy you; because Yahweh hears your murmurings which you murmur against him. And who are we? Your murmurings are not against us, but against Yahweh." Moses said to Aaron, "Tell all the congregation of the children of Israel, 'Come near before Yahweh, for he has heard your murmurings.'" It happened, as Aaron spoke to the whole congregation of the children of Israel, that they looked toward the wilderness, and behold, the glory of Yahweh appeared in the cloud. Yahweh spoke to Moses, saying, "I have heard the murmurings of the children of Israel. Speak to them, saying, 'At evening you shall eat meat, and in the morning you shall be filled with bread: and you shall know that I am Yahweh your God.' It happened at evening that quail came up and covered the camp; and in the morning the dew lay around the camp. When the dew that lay had gone, behold, on the surface of the wilderness was a small round thing, small as the frost on the ground. When the children of Israel saw it, they said one to another, "What is it?" For they didn't know what it was. Moses said to them, "It is the bread which Yahweh has given you to eat." This is the thing which Yahweh has commanded: "Gather of it everyone according to his eating; an *omer* a head, according to the number of your persons, you shall take it, every man for those who are in his tent" (Exodus 16:4-16).

They were told to gather an *omer* per head. That would be enough for each person to eat. "The children of Israel did so, and gathered some more, some less" (Exodus 4:17).

That's to be expected, isn't it? Our family goes berry picking in the blackberry patch. We never all pick the same amount. With the people of Israel, even though they were all told to pick up an *omer*—some picked up over an *omer*, and some picked up under an *omer*. But "when they measured it with an *omer*, he who gathered much had nothing over, and he who gathered little had no lack. They gathered every man according to his eating" (Exodus 4:18).

This was a miracle, not only in the giving of the manna, but in the measuring of the manna. Everybody had just enough.

Why did Yahweh do that?

Ultimately it was Yahweh God who provided the manna. The manna did not come down because of the work of the people. Even when the people picked it up, Yahweh determined how much they had. And He determined that each person had enough!

Enough was all they needed.

Laura Ingalls Wilder wrote the *Little House* books, such as *The Little House on the Prairie.* Her books are filled with folksy proverbs that people learned back then. One of Laura's mother's sayings was, "Enough is as good as a feast."

Is that right?

If you have enough, are you better off if you have still more?

You might think you will be better off to have more, because then you can lay up some for the future. But if you have enough now, and you are also guaranteed to have enough at all points in the future, is more better, or a burden?

This small example of the manna is critical to understanding Yahweh's thinking on economics. If He gives you enough, and He guarantees to always do that, why do you need more?

If you don't have to have more, and you are satisfied with enough, then you will feel free to share what you do have. Paul said:

> My friends, we want you to know that the churches in Macedonia have shown others how kind God is. Although they were going through hard times and were very poor, they were glad to give generously. They gave as much as they could afford and even more, simply because they wanted to. They even asked and begged us to let them have the joy of giving their money for God's people. And they did more than we had hoped. They gave themselves first to the Lord and then to us, just as God wanted them to do. Titus was the one who got you started doing this good thing, so we begged him to have you finish what you had begun. You do everything better than anyone else. You have stronger faith. You speak better and know more. You are eager to give, and you love us better. Now you must give more generously than

anyone else. I am not ordering you to do this. I am simply testing how real your love is by comparing it with the concern that others have shown. You know that our Lord Jesus Christ was kind enough to give up all his riches and become poor, so that you could become rich. A year ago you were the first ones to give, and you gave because you wanted to. So listen to my advice. I think you should finish what you started. If you give according to what you have, you will prove that you are as eager to give as you were to think about giving. It doesn't matter how much you have. What matters is how much you are willing to give from what you have. I am not trying to make life easier for others by making life harder for you. But it is only fair for you to share with them when you have so much, and they have so little. Later, when they have more than enough, and you are in need, they can share with you. Then everyone will have a fair share, just as the Scriptures say, "Those who gathered too much had nothing left. Those who gathered only a little had all they needed" (2 Corinthians 8:1-15, CEV).

Paul said, "It doesn't matter how much you have. What matters is how much you are willing to give from what you have."

> [Christ] looked up, and saw the rich people who were putting their gifts into the treasury. He saw a certain poor widow casting in two small brass coins. He said, "Truly I tell you, this poor widow put in more than all of them, for all these put in gifts for God from their abundance, but she, out of her poverty, put in all that she had to live on" (Luke 21:1-4).

Would any of you have done what Christ did?

Financially, the widow's mites, as they are called in the King James Version, did not matter at all to the Temple treasury. The smallest coin that the Jews used was a *prutah*— so small that the rabbis ruled that no one could give less than two *prutahs* to the temple treasury. In the rabbis' minds, one just wasn't worth the trouble and such a small gift may have insulted God. The poor widow could not give less than two *prutahs*, yet two was all she had. She gave it all. And such a small amount made no real difference to the Temple treasury.

But it did to God. Christ did not rail at her for giving everything. He loved her because she did. She was a financial failure and a spiritual success.

Now—after giving her last two mites, do you think that widow died from starvation? Or did a mighty Hand replace those mites, and more?

Again—if you have enough, and you are guaranteed that you will always have enough, why not give away part of what you have?

And if you have enough, why is more better? The key to giving is remembering Who gives you what you have.

Everything in our society says that the more you have, the better off you are. People who don't try to get a lot more are looked at as lacking ambition for not trying to get ahead.

Some Israelites laid up some manna. "Moses said to them, 'Let no one leave of it until the morning.' Notwithstanding they didn't listen to Moses, but some of them left of it until the morning, and it bred worms, and became foul: and Moses was angry with them" (Exodus 16:19-20).

Okay, so why did some of them leave it until the morning? What were they doing? Surely some were saving it. Not all, I am sure. Some were just too indolent to get rid of it. But I am also sure some wanted to get a bit ahead, and they diligently saved some manna.

What difference would it have made if they had saved manna from day to day? Why did God tell them not to save manna?

Then they would have been looking to themselves for their daily bread, instead of looking to God. "After this manner therefore pray ye: Our Father which art in heaven, Hallowed be thy name. Thy kingdom come. Thy will be done in earth, as it is in heaven. Give us this day our daily bread. And forgive us our debts, as we forgive our debtors" (Matthew 6:9-12, KJV).

Give us this day our daily bread, Y'shua said. That's not Israel in the wilderness. That's us now. *Father, give us this day our daily bread. One* omer *of manna, please. Hold the onions.*

Then, right after that, Y'shua said, "Forgive us our debts, as we forgive our debtors." When you remember where your manna or your daily bread comes from, you will remember to give some away. When you remember where your spiritual forgiveness comes from, you will remember to give some away:

> They gathered it morning by morning, everyone according to his eating. When the sun grew hot, it melted. It happened that on the sixth day they gathered twice as much bread, two *omers* for each one, and all the rulers of the congregation came and told Moses. He said to them, "This is that which Yahweh has spoken, 'Tomorrow is a solemn rest, a holy Sabbath to Yahweh. Bake that which you want to bake, and boil that which you want to boil; and all that remains over lay up for yourselves to be kept until the morning.'" They laid it up until the morning, as Moses asked, and it didn't become foul, neither was there any worm in it. Moses said, "Eat that today, for today is a Sabbath to Yahweh. Today you shall not find it in the field. Six days you shall gather it, but on the seventh day is the Sabbath. In it there shall be none." It happened on the seventh day that some of the people went out to gather, and they found none. Yahweh said to Moses, "How long do you refuse to keep my commandments and my laws? Behold, because Yahweh has given you the Sabbath, therefore he gives you on the sixth day the bread of two days. Everyone stay in his place. Let no one go out of his place on the seventh day." So the people rested on the seventh day. The house of Israel called its name *manna*, and it was like coriander seed, white; and its taste was like wafers with honey (Exodus 16:21-31).

God purposely prevented them from saving manna. On Friday, they were specifically instructed to save a day's manna so they wouldn't have to work on the Sabbath. But beyond saving for that one day, they could not store up manna.

Why did they need to? They had open access to the big Mannafacturer! For forty years, each person had an *omer* of manna. Guaranteed.

This all happened soon after Israel had left Egypt. They were not in the Holy Land yet. They still traveled through the wilderness. But the same economic principle of the giving of the manna was to guide them once they were set up in their own country. That is—they were guaranteed to have enough. And that was enough.

CHAPTER 5

SETTING UP THE HOMESTEAD

N o *debt?* No taxes? No way! The whole earth is God's. He made it. "In the beginning God created the heaven and the earth" (Genesis 1:1, KJV). Since it's His, he can do with it as He sees best. Such as during Noah's flood, when He gave it a thorough cleaning.

After Israel left Egypt, Yahweh gave them the land of Canaan; Canaan was Noah's grandson. Some will say that Israel had no right to the land of Canaan, since Canaan was there first. Canaan was there first only because God put him there. When Canaan disobeyed his Creator, the Creator kicked him out.

God can do that. It's His earth. "The earth is Yahweh's, with its fullness; the world, and those who dwell therein" (Psalms 24:1). When Yahweh finally brought Israel into the Holy Land, He gave each family their own piece of land. They did not owe a mortgage on that land. It was theirs free and clear to use, as long as they obeyed its true owner, God Himself.

Again, they owed no debt on their land.

With the recent financial crisis in the United States, it has been said that the status symbol of choice has changed from a BMW to a mortgage-free home.

Look at the way God looks at making debt:

> But if a man is just, and does that which is lawful and
> right, and has not eaten on the mountains, neither has
> lifted up his eyes to the idols of the house of Israel, neither
> has defiled his neighbor's wife, neither has come near to a

woman in her impurity, and has not wronged any, but has restored to the debtor his pledge, has taken nothing by robbery, has given his bread to the hungry, and has covered the naked with a garment; he who has not given forth on interest, neither has taken any increase, who has withdrawn his hand from iniquity, has executed true justice between man and man, has walked in my statutes, and has kept my ordinances, to deal truly; he is just, he shall surely live, says the Lord Yahweh (Ezekial 18:5-9).

Let's see now. In that passage God equates taking increase by interest with: idolatry—lifted up his eyes to the idols of the house of Israel; adultery—defiled his neighbor's wife; and robbery—taken nothing by robbery.

Now that's quite a contrast with today's thinking—debt, or credit, is viewed as a stimulus to the economy and a benefit to people.

Do you recall when double knit—polyester—was a new thing? About that time, 1973, I remember a suit salesman from India showing us "triple knit suits." You see, if double knit was good, triple knit had to be 50 percent better. In talking with that salesman, we asked him what the biggest difference was between the U.S. and India. He said the biggest difference was credit. In the U.S. you could get money to build houses or start businesses because of the availability of credit, or debt.

In many ways, access to credit, or debt, would seem to be a blessing, not a curse. We often hear how important it is to maintain a good credit rating to protect your ability to go into debt. People buy homes with debt. Almost no one pays cash for his home. On the other hand, "The rich rule over the poor. The borrower is servant to the lender" (Proverbs 22:7). If the borrower is servant to the lender, how is that true with a home mortgage?

Almost everyone who buys a home does so with a mortgage. They generally commit to twenty to thirty years of debt, which covers a major part of their working lifetime. People consider it a great blessing to be able to get a mortgage to buy a home.

How can it be that if a person takes out a thirty-year mortgage to buy a home, he is a servant to the lender? God's proverb is not going to be wrong, is it?

In addition to no mortgage debt, when Israel went into the Holy Land, there were no taxes to pay. Yahweh Himself was their king and He didn't demand taxes, as all other kings do.

God predicted that they would get tired of having a king who did not levy a tax burden on them, so He gave instructions for when they would have kings:

> When you are come to the land which Yahweh your God gives you, and shall possess it, and shall dwell therein, and shall say, I will set a king over me, like all the nations that are around me; you shall surely set him king over yourselves, whom Yahweh your God shall choose: one from among your brothers you shall set king over you; you may not put a foreigner over you, who is not your brother. Only he shall not multiply horses to himself, nor cause the people to return to Egypt, to the end that he may multiply horses; because Yahweh has said to you, You shall henceforth return no more that way. Neither shall he multiply wives to himself, that his heart not turn away: neither shall he greatly multiply to himself silver and gold (Deuteronomy 17:14-17).

The king was not to multiply wealth. When they did actually want a human king, Yahweh told them what he would do:

> Samuel told all the words of Yahweh to the people who asked of him a king. He said, This will be the manner of the king who shall reign over you: he will take your sons, and appoint them to him, for his chariots, and to be his horsemen; and they shall run before his chariots; and he will appoint them to him for captains of thousands, and captains of fifties; and he will set some to plow his ground, and to reap his harvest, and to make his instruments of war, and the instruments of his chariots. He will take your daughters to be perfumers, and to be cooks, and to be bakers. He will take your fields, and your vineyards, and your olive groves, even the best of them, and give them to his servants. He will take the tenth of your seed, and of

your vineyards, and give to his officers, and to his servants. He will take your male servants, and your female servants, and your best young men, and your donkeys, and put them to his work. He will take the tenth of your flocks: and you shall be his servants (1 Samuel 8:10-17).

The king would:

- Take their sons;
- Take their daughters;
- Take their fields, vineyards, and olive groves;
- Take a tenth of their seed and vineyards;
- Take their servants and animals; and
- Take a tenth of their flocks.

In other words, the king would oppress them with taxes. When they first went into the land, though, in the time of the judges, Yahweh was their king, and they paid no taxes.

They did have to pay tithes, or tenths, on their increase:

- Temple tithe, to those who kept the temple service going;
- Festival tithe, which they ate themselves at the festivals; and
- Poor tithe, which they paid two years out of seven, to help the poor.

But these tithes still benefitted them. The Temple tithe came back to them because it kept the Temple worship going, which was for their benefit. When the Temple was closed up, the nation suffered terribly. The festival tithe was for their enjoyment at the festivals. And the poor tithe was a welfare system which could help them all, if they needed it.

These tithes were only on increase. Some taxes are paid on increase. Some taxes, though, such as property taxes, are levied regardless of whether or not there is increase or income. One of the cruelest taxes in the United States is the property tax, generally levied to finance the bloated bureaucracy of the government public schools. Public school spending never stops going up, and property taxes keep going up. Sometimes the elderly, who have no children in the schools, are forced out of their homes by the public school tax.

So Israel had no mortgage debt and no taxes. Plus Yahweh promised Israel abundant blessing:

> If you walk in my statutes, and keep my commandments, and do them; then I will give you your rains in their season, and the land shall yield its increase, and the trees of the field shall yield their fruit. Your threshing shall reach to the vintage, and the vintage shall reach to the sowing time; and you shall eat your bread to the full, and dwell in your land safely (Leviticus 26:3-5).

They were promised such huge harvests that sowing time would come again before they could put it up. Their barns would be full. After all, they were in the land of milk and honey:

> Then our sons will be like well-nurtured plants, our daughters like pillars carved to adorn a palace. Our barns are full, filled with all kinds of provision. Our sheep bring forth thousands and ten thousands in our fields. Our oxen will pull heavy loads. There is no breaking in, and no going away, and no outcry in our streets. Happy are the people who are in such a situation. Happy are the people whose God is Yahweh (Psalms 144:12-15).

Israel had everything they needed. No debt, no taxes, abundant crops. Just as in the wilderness, they had their *omer* of manna. They had enough, and that was plenty.

However, because they had enough, that was not to be used as a basis for getting more, or accumulating wealth, or getting rich. Because they had enough, that was the very reason they did not have to spend their time on endless accumulation. "A man in a crowd said to Jesus, 'Teacher, tell my brother to give me my share of what our father left us when he died.' Jesus answered, 'Who gave me the right to settle arguments between you and your brother?'" (Luke 12:13-14, CEV). The man complained that his brother had cheated him out of his rightful inheritance. Jesus or Y'shua did not jump on the brother who had committed the crime, but reproached the man who had the King of God's kingdom right in front of him, yet he was only thinking about wealth.

Think about that. Christ had healed many, some were even raised from the dead, words came from His mouth the likes of which the world had never heard—and this guy thinks, "Hey, maybe He can help me get my property back!"

Priorities!

Christ went on:

> Then he said to the crowd, "Don't be greedy! Owning a lot of things won't make your life safe." So Jesus told them this story: A rich man's farm produced a big crop, and he said to himself, "What can I do? I don't have a place large enough to store everything." Later he said, "Now I know what I'll do. I'll tear down my barns and build bigger ones, where I can store all my grain and other goods. Then I'll say to myself, 'You have stored up enough good things to last for years to come. Live it up! Eat, drink, and enjoy yourself.'" But God said to him, "You fool! Tonight you will die. Then who will get what you have stored up?" This is what happens to people who store up everything for themselves, but are poor in the sight of God (Luke 12:15-21, CEV).

Israel was in this rich man's shoes. They had plenty. No debt, no taxes, and so much harvest they could scarcely get it in before it was time to plant more.

The rich man's barns were full, yet he wanted still bigger barns. He said he wanted more wealth so he could then stop accumulating wealth, but that usually does not happen. "If you love money, you will never be satisfied; if you long to be rich, you will never get all you want. It is useless" (Ecclesiastes 5:10, GNB).

Accumulating is addictive. The more you get, th
want. You may not need more, but you will
anyway. That becomes who you are. The rich m
bigger barns was not looking to sustain himself. He was looking
to exalt himself. He was not looking for his daily bread from
God. He was looking to be his own god. "To whom will you
liken me, and make me equal, and compare me, that we may be
like? Some pour out gold from the bag, and weigh silver in the
balance. They hire a goldsmith, and he makes it a god. They fall
down—yes, they worship" (Isaiah 46:5-6).

This is what happens. Not just the gold being made into a
physical idol, but the gold itself becomes an idol:

> Jesus said to his disciples: I tell you not to worry about
> your life! Don't worry about having something to eat or
> wear. Life is more than food or clothing. Look at the
> crows! They don't plant or harvest, and they don't have
> storehouses or barns. But God takes care of them. You are
> much more important than any birds. Can worry make
> you live longer? If you don't have power over small
> things, why worry about everything else? Look how the
> wild flowers grow! They don't work hard to make their
> clothes. But I tell you that Solomon with all his wealth
> wasn't as well clothed as one of these flowers. God gives
> such beauty to everything that grows in the fields, even
> though it is here today and thrown into a fire tomorrow.
> Won't he do even more for you? You have such little faith!
> Don't keep worrying about having something to eat or
> drink. Only people who don't know God are always
> worrying about such things. Your Father knows what you
> need. But put God's work first, and these things will be
> yours as well. My little group of disciples, don't be afraid!
> Your Father wants to give you the kingdom. Sell what you
> have and give the money to the poor. Make yourselves
> moneybags that never wear out. Make sure your treasure
> is safe in heaven, where thieves cannot steal it and moths
> cannot destroy it. Your heart will always be where your
> treasure is (Luke 12, 22-34, CEV).

Your heart will always be where your treasure is. If a person has enough, he only needs to accumulate more if he does not believe that God will continue to give him enough. Israel only needed to hoard manna if they thought that God would not send more manna tomorrow.

Accumulating physical wealth takes great effort. It is not easy. It is the most competitive game on earth.

Accumulating wealth takes time. Time is life. No one has much of that. No one knows just how much he does have.

> My days pass by without hope, pass faster than a weaver's shuttle. Remember, O God, my life is only a breath (Job 7:6-7, GNB).

> Yahweh, show me my end, what is the measure of my days. Let me know how frail I am. Behold, you have made my days handbreadths. My lifetime is as nothing before you. Surely every man stands as a breath. *Selah.* Surely every man walks like a shadow. Surely they busy themselves in vain. He heaps up, and doesn't know who shall gather. Now, Lord, what do I wait for? My hope is in you (Psalms 39:4-7).

> Come now, you who say, "Today or tomorrow we will go into such and such a town and spend a year there and trade and make a profit"—yet you do not know what tomorrow will bring. What is your life? For you are a mist that appears for a little time and then vanishes. Instead you ought to say, "If the Lord wills, we will live and do this or that." As it is, you boast in your arrogance. All such boasting is evil (James 4:13-16, ESV).

Life is like a pass of a weaver's shuttle. *Click.* Or a breath. *Poof.* Or a morning mist, gone before noon. If life is so short, then those who heap up busy themselves in vain. "Do not lay up for yourselves treasures on earth, where moth and rust destroy and where thieves break in and steal, but lay up for yourselves treasures in heaven, where neither moth nor rust destroys and where thieves do not break in and steal" (Matthew 6:19-20, ESV).

When Israel was in the wilderness and some heaped up extra manna, the very next day it rotted. They had a manna mess. It stank and bred worms. That happened quickly, in one day. They saw it. They smelled it. They had to squash the worms, and it was yucky when they squished. That also squashed their heaping. They stopped hoarding manna. They could quickly see that it rotted. Why in the world would they spend half the morning picking up extra manna when it was going to be rotten the very next day?

If people could only learn that life lesson so quickly.

Heaped wealth also rots. It takes a person's life, and rots his soul. When this short day of life passes, and we each stand to be judged by Christ, heaped wealth will be no better than stinking, wormy manna. We will all see that then.

Few see it now:

> Come, everyone who thirsts, come to the waters; and he who has no money, come, buy and eat! Come, buy wine and milk without money and without price. Why do you spend your money for that which is not bread, and your labor for that which does not satisfy? Listen diligently to me, and eat what is good, and delight yourselves in rich food. Incline your ear, and come to me; hear, that your soul may live; and I will make with you an everlasting covenant, my steadfast, sure love for David (Isaiah 55:1-3, ESV).

Israel had no debt, no taxes, and enough to live on. That was not to be used as a base for heaping up wealth. That was why they did not need to.

CHAPTER 6

LIVING THE GOOD LIFE—THE SABBATH

Israel was in the land. Yahweh set them up with no debt, no taxes, and everything they needed.

What was everything they needed?

Him.

When they had wandered in the wilderness and had received manna for forty years, it wasn't the manna that had brought them through. Yahweh God brought them through.

When He brought them into the land of milk and honey, it wasn't the milk and honey that would see them through. Yahweh God was their support.

No debt, no taxes, and everything they needed.

Then what?

Which is to say—if a person does not need to spend his life accumulating wealth, then what in the world would he do with his time?

There was absolutely no physical reason for them to waste their lives trying to accumulate wealth because they were promised all the wealth they would ever need.

So what in the world would people do with their lives?

Normally, people spend all their lives trying to "get ahead." They go to work full time in their early twenties. Mothers used to work full time in the home, but now most women work away from home. Which means that home ain't nearly the home that it used to be, and about twice as many of those homes break apart. They don't have a homemaker.

We work full time for forty-five to fifty years, getting a couple of weeks off every year, never getting a year off from our jobs. Most people dislike their jobs, and spend those forty-five years wishing they were doing something else.

Communist China has recently joined the capitalist economies, although still retaining, for the time being, its communist government. However, now that the people are free to work at what they want to work at instead of on a collective farm, they are still not satisfied. A ten-year nationwide survey found that almost all Chinese dislike their jobs:

> For the last decade [1994-2004], the Gallup Organization has surveyed the people of China, as both consumers of goods and employees of the companies that produce those goods.
>
> The survey found that 68 percent of Chinese employees don't approach their work with passion or feel a personal connection to their jobs. These employees have essentially checked out; they are sleepwalking through their workdays. And a further 20 percent of employees hate their jobs to the point of active disengagement. When 88 percent of employees in China aren't interested in their jobs, productivity suffers—even in a mass-production assembly-line culture.[1]

Ehow.com lists these guidelines to tell if you hate your job so much that it is making you sick:

- Observe that you feel stressed most of the time, rather than being happy and comfortable with your work.

- See that you suffer from either mild or severe depression, and you take the depression home with you.

- Wonder why you have lost interest in being noticed by management or making a significant contribution to the company.

- Notice that you find your work so boring that you don't even want to do it.

- Realize that you always feel exhausted and are having problems sleeping.

- Diagnose that you are getting more headaches and colds.[2]

People who don't really like what they are spending their lives doing, which is most people, console themselves by focusing on their retirement accounts and looking forward to the time when they will finally be able to retire and do what they really want to do. That's the greatest proof that people dislike their jobs. When they get the chance to retire and leave those jobs, most do it as soon as possible.

That's the story of most lives. Work all your life at something you'd rather not be doing, and save up for the time when you don't have to do that, anymore. That is called "getting ahead."

It's also called "the rat race."

What is a rat race?

A rat is in a cage. He can't get out of the cage and he knows it. His whole life is caged boredom, without meaning and without escape. The rat gets on his toy, a vertical wheel that goes 'round and 'round as he runs on it. Running 'round that wheel does not get the rat out of his cage. No matter how fast he runs, it does not get the rat anywhere. But it makes the rat feel as if he is going somewhere.

That's the rat race.

This chapter is titled "Living the Good Life." What does that phrase usually mean?

To live the good life normally means that you are on easy street, and that you have enough wealth to take it easy, to indulge yourself, and to get to do what you want. In other words, living the good life is selfish.

The real good life is not selfish. Really living the good life is doing good, not for yourself, but for God and others.

According to the natural law of the two great commandments, living the good life is serving God and others. That is the only way to be really happy and fulfilled. Serving self will make you unhappy. Serving God and others will make you happy.

So what would God have the people of Israel do, once He put them in His land, without debt, without taxes, and with everything they needed?

He would have them use their lives to live the two great commandments—to love God and others.

Remember when Yahweh gave Israel the manna in the wilderness? The manna fell on six days. Any manna left until the next day rotted. Except on the sixth day they got a double amount and saved it for the seventh day. That saved Sabbath manna did not rot.

For forty years manna fell on the first, second, third, fourth, fifth, and sixth days, and on the Sabbath it did not fall. That was quite a lesson, setting apart the seventh day.

The seventh day is a memorial of creation. When a builder builds something, he usually puts a sign on it saying that he built it. The Sabbath, ending the seven-day week, is God's sign on His creation. The year is based on the sun. The month is based on the moon. The seven-day week ending with the Sabbath is only based on God's giving it. There is no astronomical reason for the seven-day week, but it is followed all around the earth, and always has been.

The Sabbath commandment is the fourth of the Ten Commandments:

> Remember the Sabbath day, to keep it holy. You shall labor six days, and do all your work, but the seventh day is a Sabbath to Yahweh your God. You shall not do any work in it, you, nor your son, nor your daughter, your male servant, nor your female servant, nor your livestock, nor your stranger who is within your gates; for in six days Yahweh made heaven and earth, the sea, and all that is in them, and rested the seventh day; therefore Yahweh blessed the Sabbath day, and made it holy (Exodus 20:8-11).

Part of this commandment is to work six days, just as when God gave the manna for six days. Then on the seventh day, no one was to do ordinary work, because Yahweh made the Sabbath day holy at creation.

The Sabbath day, then, is fulfilling the first great commandment to love God:

> If you turn away your foot from the Sabbath, from doing your pleasure on my holy day; and call the Sabbath a delight, and the holy of Yahweh honorable; and shall honor it, not doing your own ways, nor finding your own pleasure, nor speaking your own words: then you shall delight yourself in Yahweh; and I will make you to ride on the high places of the earth; and I will feed you with the heritage of Jacob your father for the mouth of Yahweh has spoken it (Isaiah 58:13-14).

> If you turn your foot because of the Sabbath, from doing what you please on My holy days, and call the Sabbath a delight, the holy of Jehovah, honorable; and shall honor Him, not doing your own ways, nor finding your own pleasure, nor speaking your own words, then you shall delight yourself in Jehovah; and I will cause you to ride on the high places of the earth, and feed yourself with the inheritance of Jacob your father. For the mouth of Jehovah has spoken (Isaiah 58:13-14, MKJV).

Notice that the Sabbath was to be a delight, not a burden: "call the Sabbath a delight." The joy of the Sabbath was "to delight yourself in Yahweh."

Six days were to be spent working. The seventh day was to take delight in visiting with your Father. "Also delight yourself in Yahweh, and he will give you the desires of your heart" (Psalms 37:4). "Yahweh's works are great, pondered by all those who delight in them" (Psalms 111:2).

The Jewish theologians made the Sabbath not a delight, but a burden of bureaucratic rules. They thought that by adding their many points, they made the Sabbath more sacred. But they missed the point.

On the last day of each week, Israel was totally to forsake their normal doings for more important matters. *The Bible in Basic English* says in Isaiah 58:13: "[G]ive respect to him by not doing your business, or going after your pleasure, or saying unholy words." They were not to do their business, or their recreation, or even talk about such ordinary stuff. The Sabbath was God time.

How can a person stand it, if on the Sabbath, he is not to work, recreate, or even dwell on such things? Is that an oppressive day or what? It's no wonder Judaism made all their legal restrictions to try to force people to obey the Sabbath. Most did not want to do that.

The only way that a person could enjoy the Sabbath was if they actually delighted in being with God.

On the other hand, if a person actually delighted in being with God, delighted in considering His works, delighted in having time off from the rigor and all consuming passion of making a living— then the Sabbath would be an enormous blessing.

Part of the really good life.

The Sabbath was one-seventh of their lives. Fourteen percent.

That's quite a bit.

What would they do on the Sabbath?

If they couldn't do their work, and they couldn't do their play, and they couldn't even let their minds dwell on their work and their play, what in the world would they do?

That's like our previous question about life, isn't it? If people don't spend their lives trying to make money, what is there left to do?

What would they do on the Sabbath?

Well, they could get close to God on His set time.

Leviticus 23 lists the feasts of Yahweh. The Sabbath is the first one:

> Yahweh spoke to Moses, saying, "Speak to the children of
> Israel, and tell them, 'The set feasts of Yahweh, which you
> shall proclaim to be holy convocations, even these are my

> set feasts. Six days shall work be done: but on the seventh
> day is a Sabbath of solemn rest, a holy convocation; you
> shall do no manner of work. It is a Sabbath to Yahweh in
> all your dwellings'" (Leviticus 23:1-3).

The word given as "set feasts" is *moed*, which means a set time,
as in: "But my covenant will I establish with Isaac, which
Sarah shall bear unto thee at this *set time* in the next year"
(Genesis 17:21, KJV). The word *moed* was Sarah's set time. The
feasts are God's set times. He set them.

When Israel couldn't work, play, or even want to on the
Sabbath—they could get close to Yahweh on His set time.
After all, that's why He set it: to delight in Him.

Most people aren't comfortable with God. Just God.

Even those who might be comfortable in church or a
religious meeting with other people are not usually comfortable
just with God. If there is no noise, then there must not be
anything going on.

Notice this contrast between the righteous and the wicked:
"And the work of righteousness shall be peace; and the service
of righteousness shall be quietness and hope forever" (Isaiah
32:17, MKJV). "But the wicked are like the troubled sea, which
cannot rest, and its waters cast up mire and dirt. There is no
peace, says my God, to the wicked" (Isaiah 57: 20-21, MKJV).
The righteous have quiet peace. The wicked cannot rest. God
is found more in quiet times than noisy.

Anna lived an unusual life. She didn't do "nothing." God
thought so much of Anna that when His little boy was born,
He made a special point to show Him to Anna:

> And when the time came for their purification according
> to the Law of Moses, they brought him (the Christ child)
> up to Jerusalem to present him to the Lord…. And there
> was a prophetess, Anna, the daughter of Phanuel, of the
> tribe of Asher. She was advanced in years, having lived
> with her husband seven years from when she was a
> virgin, and then as a widow until she was eighty-four. She
> did not depart from the temple, worshiping with fasting

and prayer night and day. And coming up at that very
hour she began to give thanks to God and to speak of him
to all who were waiting for the redemption of Jerusalem
(Luke 2:22, 36-38, ESV).

As a young widow, Anna had lost her love, her husband. But she
had another love. She doted on Him. She dedicated her life to
Him. She spent as much time as she possibly could with Him.

Anna didn't do nothing. It appeared to others that she did
nothing—never leaving the temple, spending all her time
praying and fasting. Notice that she was not content just to
spend her time praying, but she also fasted. Why did she fast,
when she spent all her time with God anyway? Because
fasting humbled her more and she could get still closer to God.
That which kept her from God was herself. Fasting removed
some of that.

Anna was one hungry lady! Not for food, but for God. She
doted on God and was devoted to Him. Doted and devoted!

No, Anna didn't do nothing. She did everything that is
most valuable in life to do. She loved God.

The Sabbath was given to do nothing, and to do
everything in life that is most valuable to do—spend time with
God. One-seventh of your life, to be specific. Fourteen percent.

The Sabbath commandment was not a commandment to
prevent people from doing what they really wanted to do—
business and recreation. The Sabbath commandment was to
give us time to do that which we really, really want to do—
delight in Yahweh.

But there are always some who don't appreciate that and
can't get their minds off the manna, even for one day:

It happened that on the sixth day they gathered twice as
much bread, two *omers* for each one, and all the rulers of
the congregation came and told Moses. He said to them,
"This is that which Yahweh has spoken, 'Tomorrow is a
solemn rest, a holy Sabbath to Yahweh. Bake that which
you want to bake, and boil that which you want to boil;
and all that remains over lay up for yourselves to be kept

until the morning.'" They laid it up until the morning, as Moses asked, and it didn't become foul, neither was there any worm in it. Moses said, "Eat that today, for today is a Sabbath to Yahweh. Today you shall not find it in the field. Six days you shall gather it, but on the seventh day is the Sabbath. In it there shall be none." It happened on the seventh day that some of the people went out to gather, and they found none. Yahweh said to Moses, "How long do you refuse to keep my commandments and my laws? Behold, because Yahweh has given you the Sabbath, therefore he gives you on the sixth day the bread of two days. Everyone stay in his place. Let no one go out of his place on the seventh day." So the people rested on the seventh day (Exodus 16:22-30).

Israel didn't have to work seven days a week. They had a day off, with pay. But that day had a purpose. That was a feast day to gorge on God. One-seventh of their lives was to be spent gorging on God. That is the good life.

CHAPTER 7

NINETEEN DAYS OF FEASTS

The word "feast" sounds, well, kind of bad. Like the infamous Roman feasts during which Romans stuffed themselves then forced themselves to throw it up. So they could feast some more.

That does sound kind of bad!

Oddly enough, many people think God's feasts are bad. Must be that word "feast."

But God does have feasts:

> You shall observe a feast to me three times a year. You shall observe the feast of unleavened bread. Seven days you shall eat unleavened bread, as I commanded you, at the time appointed in the month Abib (for in it you came out from Egypt), and no one shall appear before me empty. And the feast of harvest, the first fruits of your labors, which you sow in the field: and the feast of harvest, at the end of the year, when you gather in your labors out of the field. Three times in the year all your males shall appear before the Lord Yahweh (Exodus 23: 14-17).

When Yahweh set up Israel in the Holy Land, He commanded the males to go to the feasts three times a year.

Now when most people lived agriculturally, and everybody left, somebody had to stay home to take care of the animals. That's just the way it is down on the farm. Animals always need tending.

Actually, though, not just the males went to the feasts, but most everybody did. As in this example of Y'shua and his family:

Now his parents went to Jerusalem every year at the Feast of the Passover. And when he was twelve years old, they went up according to custom. And when the feast was ended, as they were returning, the boy Jesus stayed behind in Jerusalem. His parents did not know it, but supposing him to be in the group they went a day's journey, but then they began to search for him among their relatives and acquaintances, and when they did not find him, they returned to Jerusalem, searching for him. After three days they found him in the temple, sitting among the teachers, listening to them and asking them questions. And all who heard him were amazed at his understanding and his answers. And when his parents saw him, they were astonished. And his mother said to him, "Son, why have you treated us so? Behold, your father and I have been searching for you in great distress." And he said to them, "Why were you looking for me? Did you not know that I must be in my Father's house?" And they did not understand the saying that he spoke to them. And he went down with them and came to Nazareth and was submissive to them. And his mother treasured up all these things in her heart (Luke 2:41-51, ESV).

The whole family was there. Not just the immediate family, but the extended family. Aunts, uncles, and cousins in the caravan headed up to Jerusalem for Yahweh's festival!

Three times a year!

Most people today take some kind of vacation once a year. But three times a year? That's not realistic.

The three festival seasons consisted of eight days around the spring equinox, then one day seven weeks later as the weather really warms up, and then the seventh month around the fall equinox, when the growing is over:

These are the set feasts of Yahweh, even holy convocations, which you shall proclaim in their appointed season. In the first month, on the fourteenth day of the month in the evening, is Yahweh's Passover. On the fifteenth day of the same month is the feast of unleavened bread to Yahweh. Seven days you shall eat unleavened bread.

You shall count from the next day after the Sabbath, from the day that you brought the sheaf of the wave offering; seven Sabbaths shall be completed: even to the next day after the seventh Sabbath you shall number fifty days; and you shall offer a new meal offering to Yahweh.

Speak to the children of Israel, saying, "In the seventh month, on the first day of the month, shall be a solemn rest to you, a memorial of blowing of trumpets, a holy convocation.

"However on the tenth day of this seventh month is the day of atonement: it shall be a holy convocation to you, and you shall afflict yourselves; and you shall offer an offering made by fire to Yahweh. You shall do no manner of work in that same day; for it is a day of atonement, to make atonement for you before Yahweh your God. For whoever it is who shall not deny himself in that same day; shall be cut off from his people. Whoever it is who does any manner of work in that same day, that person I will destroy from among his people. You shall do no manner of work: it is a statute forever throughout your generations in all your dwellings. It shall be a Sabbath of solemn rest for you, and you shall deny yourselves. In the ninth day of the month at evening, from evening to evening, you shall keep your Sabbath." Yahweh spoke to Moses, saying, "Speak to the children of Israel, and say, 'On the fifteenth day of this seventh month is the feast of tents for seven days to Yahweh. On the first day shall be a holy convocation: you shall do no regular work. Seven days you shall offer an offering made by fire to Yahweh. On the eighth day shall be a holy convocation to you; and you shall offer an offering made by fire to Yahweh. It is a solemn assembly; you shall do no regular work'" (Leviticus 23: 4-6, 15-16, 24, 27-36).

In sum, the three festival seasons were: Passover and Unleavened Bread, eight days around the start of spring; Pentecost, about seven weeks later, only one day of itself; Trumpets, Atonement, and Tabernacles and the Last Day, in the fall—the first and tenth days of the seventh month and the fifteenth through the twenty-second days of that month.

So—if they kept the feasts three times a year—how did they ever get anything done?

These festivals total nineteen days. Seven days are Sabbaths, or rest days when no ordinary work is done, and twelve are common festival days. This is parallel to the cycle of the relationship of the sun and the moon, which the Bible calendar follows. The Romans went by a sun calendar. The Muslims go by a lunar calendar. The Bible festivals follow a sun and moon calendar. Every nineteen years this solar/lunar cycle of seven long years and twelve common years repeats, just as God repeated the feasts on the seven high festival days and the twelve common festival days.

In addition to the nineteen festival days, Israel had to take the time to travel to the festivals. When Christ's family traveled to the Passover festival mentioned in Luke, they had to travel about sixty miles from Nazareth to Jerusalem. That's a hard three-day journey, or perhaps more. If the average family lived forty miles from Jerusalem, that adds a couple of days' travel time on each end of the festival. Three festivals would add another dozen days' travel time to the festival time.

In other words, they spent about a month a year on the festivals.

Again—how did they ever get anything done?

Well, what was it they most needed to get done? Which is to say, what is the ultimate purpose of life?

When you reach the day of your death, what is it that you will want to have accomplished? At that time, will you hope to have gathered a lot of wealth? But what good will that do you then?

You will not be able to take it with you, you know.

The Egyptians tried that. They would bury a mummy with all sorts of things supposed to help him in the afterlife. How do we know this? Those things still sit in the tombs. In other words—the stuff did not go with the dead into the afterlife.

Remember that Yahweh had promised to bless His people with everything they needed, as long as they obeyed Him. He was everything they needed. Therefore they did not need more stuff.

With such a financial backer, they could afford to take off three times a year for the festivals.

When everybody went to the feasts, almost no one stayed behind with the stock and the stuff. The thieves of today would be in Nirvana, wouldn't they?

No, they wouldn't be in Nirvana. They would be in the Holy Land, God's land, under His watchful eye. "Yahweh's eyes are everywhere, keeping watch on the evil and the good" (Proverbs 15:3). That's the ultimate security service. Everybody was gone to the feast, almost nobody back with the stock and stuff, and nobody better touch it.

Furthermore, it wasn't just thieves the country had to worry about—ordinarily speaking. At the time of the feasts, the whole nation was humanly defenseless. All of its men were in Jerusalem. Surrounding nations could have overrun the countryside.

But when a whole nation keeps Yahweh's feasts, we are not ordinarily speaking:

> Blessed is the nation whose God is Yahweh, the people whom he has chosen for his own inheritance. Yahweh looks from heaven. He sees all the sons of men. From the place of his habitation he looks out on all the inhabitants of the earth, he who fashions all of their hearts; and he considers all of their works. There is no king saved by the multitude of an army. A mighty man is not delivered by great strength. A horse is a vain thing for safety, neither does he deliver any by his great power. Behold, Yahweh's eye is on those who fear him, on those who hope in his loving kindness; to deliver their soul from death, to keep them alive in famine. Our soul has waited for Yahweh. He is our help and our shield. For our heart rejoices in him, because we have trusted in his holy name. Let your loving kindness be on us, Yahweh, since we have hoped in you (Psalms 33:12-22).

So during the feasts the nation was totally vulnerable and totally protected. But as was Paul, when they were weakest they were strongest:

> So to keep me from becoming conceited because of the surpassing greatness of the revelations, a thorn was given me in the flesh, a messenger of Satan to harass me, to keep me from becoming conceited. Three times I pleaded with the Lord about this, that it should leave me. But he said to me, "My grace is sufficient for you, for my power is made perfect in weakness." Therefore I will boast all the more gladly of my weaknesses, so that the power of Christ may rest upon me. For the sake of Christ, then, I am content with weaknesses, insults, hardships, persecutions, and calamities. For when I am weak, then I am strong (2 Corinthians 12:7-10, ESV).

Israel held a feast to Yahweh, three times a year. These feasts were not like Roman feasts. The purpose of a Roman feast was to stuff yourself. They celebrated selfishness. Yahweh's feasts were given to rejoice before and with Him, as is described for the Feast of Tabernacles: "You shall take on the first day the fruit of goodly trees, branches of palm trees, and boughs of thick trees, and willows of the brook; and you shall rejoice before Yahweh your God seven days" (Leviticus 23:40).

> You shall keep the feast of tents seven days, after that you have gathered in from your threshing floor and from your winepress and you shall *rejoice* in your feast, you, and your son, and your daughter, and your male servant, and your female servant, and the Levite, and the foreigner, and the fatherless, and the widow, who are within your gates. You shall keep a feast to Yahweh your God seven days in the place which Yahweh shall choose; because Yahweh your God will bless you in all your increase, and in all the work of your hands, and you shall be altogether _joyful_ (Deuteronomy 16:13-15).

The biggest thing about the festivals is that God is in them. The absolute biggest events in the Bible occurred during a festival. Two of these are shown in Exodus 12. "It happened at the end of four hundred thirty years, even the same day it happened, that all the armies of Yahweh went out from the land of Egypt" (Exodus 12:41).

This is speaking of the Passover in Egypt, when the death angel passed over Israelite homes if that home's inhabitants had placed the blood of a lamb on their door. That is one of the great events in human history. However, this is also referring back to the promise made to Abraham that this would happen. That happened on the same day, four hundred and thirty years before, to the day. That covenant with Abraham was also one of the great events in the Bible, and also took place on a festival day. This shows that God's festivals did not start in Egypt.

About seven weeks after Israel left Egypt, Yahweh Himself taught the Israelites the Ten Commandments at the time of the Festival of Pentecost, or the harvest of the first fruits, as it is called in Exodus 23. Certainly when God came down on the mountain and personally taught His people His law, that was one of the great events in the Bible.

In the New Testament, Christ was sacrificed at Passover—the greatest event of all in the Bible.

And the Holy Spirit was given at Pentecost.

Those five events are critical in human history, and they all occurred on a festival. The Bible doesn't say so, but the Jews maintain that creation itself was on the Feast of Trumpets. And it may well be that the Feast of Trumpets itself looks forward to the return of the Messiah at the last trumpet.

So it seems we have seven major Biblical events happening at the time of a festival:

- Creation.
- Covenant with Abraham.
- Exodus.
- Ten Commandments.
- Christ's sacrifice.

- Holy Spirit.

- Christ's return?

The big thing about God's festivals is that God is in them. They tell His plan for mankind. The events pictured by the spring festivals have already occurred. The events pictured by the fall festivals have yet to be fulfilled.

The times of greatest closeness to God occurred during the festivals.

Solomon finished building the First Temple, after seven years of building, and Yahweh's glory came into the Temple at the time of the Feast of Tabernacles in the seventh month:

> Now when Solomon had made an end of praying, the fire came down from heaven, and consumed the burnt offering and the sacrifices; and the glory of Yahweh filled the house. The priests could not enter into the house of Yahweh, because the glory of Yahweh filled Yahweh's house. All the children of Israel looked on, when the fire came down, and the glory of Yahweh was on the house; and they bowed themselves with their faces to the ground on the pavement, and worshiped, and gave thanks to Yahweh, saying, For he is good; for his loving kindness endures for ever....

> So Solomon held the feast at that time seven days, and all Israel with him, a very great assembly, from the entrance of Hamath to the brook of Egypt. On the eighth day they held a solemn assembly: for they kept the dedication of the altar seven days, and the feast seven days. On the three and twentieth day of the seventh month he sent the people away to their tents, joyful and glad of heart for the goodness that Yahweh had shown to David, and to Solomon, and to Israel his people (2 Chronicles 7:1-3, 8-10).

God's people observed the festivals during times of great repentance and revival. For example, Ahaz, the king of Judah just before Hezekiah, did this:

Ahaz was twenty years old when he began to reign; and he reigned sixteen years in Jerusalem: and he didn't do that which was right in the eyes of Yahweh, like David his father; but he walked in the ways of the kings of Israel, and made also molten images for the Baals. Moreover he burnt incense in the valley of the son of Hinnom, and burnt his children in the fire, according to the abominations of the nations whom Yahweh cast out before the children of Israel. He sacrificed and burnt incense in the high places, and on the hills, and under every green tree. Therefore Yahweh his God delivered him into the hand of the king of Syria; and they struck him, and carried away of his a great multitude of captives, and brought them to Damascus. He was also delivered into the hand of the king of Israel, who struck him with a great slaughter....

At that time did king Ahaz send to the kings of Assyria to help him. For again the Edomites had come and struck Judah, and carried away captives. The Philistines also had invaded the cities of the lowland, and of the South of Judah, and had taken Beth Shemesh, and Aijalon, and Gederoth, and Soco with its towns, and Timnah with its towns, Gimzo also and its towns: and they lived there. For Yahweh brought Judah low because of Ahaz king of Israel; for he had dealt wantonly in Judah, and trespassed severely against Yahweh. Tilgath Pilneser king of Assyria came to him, and distressed him, but didn't strengthen him. For Ahaz took away a portion out of the house of Yahweh, and out of the house of the king and of the princes, and gave it to the king of Assyria: but it didn't help him. In the time of his distress did he trespass yet more against Yahweh, this same king Ahaz. For he sacrificed to the gods of Damascus, which struck him; and he said, Because the gods of the kings of Syria helped them, therefore will I sacrifice to them, that they may help me. But they were the ruin of him, and of all Israel. Ahaz gathered together the vessels of the house of God, and cut in pieces the vessels of the house of God, and shut up the doors of the house of Yahweh; and he made him altars in every corner of Jerusalem. In every city of Judah he made high places to burn incense to other gods, and provoked to anger Yahweh, the God of his fathers. Now the rest of his acts, and all his ways, first and last, behold, they are written in the book of the kings of Judah and Israel. Ahaz slept with his fathers, and they buried him in the city, even in Jerusalem; for they didn't bring him into the tombs of the kings of Israel: and Hezekiah his son reigned in his place (2 Chronicles 28:1-5, 16-27).

Hezekiah was not like his father Ahaz. One of the first things good King Hezekiah did was to observe Yahweh's festivals. Ahaz had shut up the doors of the house of Yahweh. Ahaz did not have time to keep the feasts:

Hezekiah sent to all Israel and Judah, and wrote letters also to Ephraim and Manasseh, that they should come to the house of Yahweh at Jerusalem, to keep the Passover to Yahweh, the God of Israel. For the king had taken counsel, and his princes, and all the assembly in Jerusalem, to keep the Passover in the second month. For they could not keep it at that time, because the priests had not sanctified themselves in sufficient number, neither had the people gathered themselves together to Jerusalem (2 Chronicles 30:1-3).

Under Ahaz, the people had gotten out of the routine of observing the holy times. So when Hezekiah became king, they could not keep the Passover in the first month. They weren't ready for it:

The thing was right in the eyes of the king and of all the assembly. So they established a decree to make proclamation throughout all Israel, from Beersheba even to Dan, that they should come to keep the Passover to Yahweh, the God of Israel, at Jerusalem: for they had not kept it in great numbers in such sort as it is written. So the posts went with the letters from the king and his princes throughout all Israel and Judah, and according to the commandment of the king, saying, You children of Israel, turn again to Yahweh, the God of Abraham, Isaac, and Israel, that he may return to the remnant that have escaped of you out of the hand of the kings of Assyria. Don't be like your fathers, and like your brothers, who trespassed against Yahweh, the God of their fathers, so that he gave them up to desolation, as you see (2 Chronicles 30:4-7).

The northern kingdom of Israel had, like the kingdom of Judah, quit keeping the festivals, and also substituted festivals of their own. This was done under Jeroboam, their first king after the split from Judah when Solomon died:

> Jeroboam said in his heart, Now will the kingdom return to the house of David: if this people go up to offer sacrifices in the house of Yahweh at Jerusalem, then will the heart of this people turn again to their lord, even to Rehoboam king of Judah; and they will kill me, and return to Rehoboam king of Judah. Whereupon the king took counsel, and made two calves of gold; and he said to them, It is too much for you to go up to Jerusalem: see your gods, Israel, which brought you up out of the land of Egypt. He set the one in Bethel, and the other put he in Dan. This thing became a sin; for the people went to worship before the one, even to Dan. He made houses of high places, and made priests from among all the people, who were not of the sons of Levi. Jeroboam ordained a feast in the eighth month, on the fifteenth day of the month, like the feast that is in Judah, and he went up to the altar; so did he in Bethel, sacrificing to the calves that he had made: and he placed in Bethel the priests of the high places that he had made. He went up to the altar which he had made in Bethel on the fifteenth day in the eighth month, even in the month which he had devised of his own heart: and he ordained a feast for the children of Israel, and went up to the altar, to burn incense (1 Kings 12:26-33).

But when Israel left Yahweh, He left them. With Him, they needed nothing else. Without Him, they had nothing. For God to be with you, you must be with Him.

Hezekiah brought Judah, and some of Israel, back to God at the Passover:

> Now don't you be stiff-necked, as your fathers were; but yield yourselves to Yahweh, and enter into his sanctuary, which he has sanctified forever, and serve Yahweh your God, that his fierce anger may turn away from you. For if you turn again to Yahweh, your brothers and your children shall find compassion before those who led them captive, and shall come again into this land: for Yahweh

your God is gracious and merciful, and will not turn away his face from you, if you return to him. So the posts passed from city to city through the country of Ephraim and Manasseh, even to Zebulun: but they ridiculed them, and mocked them (2 Chronicles 30:8-10).

They were mocked for going to Jerusalem to keep the feasts. "Nevertheless certain men of Asher and Manasseh and of Zebulun humbled themselves, and came to Jerusalem. Also on Judah came the hand of God to give them one heart, to do the commandment of the king and of the princes by the word of Yahweh" (2 Chronicles 30:11-12). Notice that God gave them the heart to do this. Once they turned to Him to keep the Passover, He gave them the spirit of the Passover:

There assembled at Jerusalem much people to keep the feast of unleavened bread in the second month, a very great assembly. They arose and took away the altars that were in Jerusalem, and all the altars for incense took they away, and cast them into the brook Kidron. Then they killed the Passover on the fourteenth day of the second month: and the priests and the Levites were ashamed, and sanctified themselves, and brought burnt offerings into the house of Yahweh. They stood in their place after their order, according to the law of Moses the man of God: the priests sprinkled the blood which they received of the hand of the Levites. For there were many in the assembly who had not sanctified themselves: therefore the Levites were in charge of killing the Passovers for everyone who was not clean, to sanctify them to Yahweh. For a multitude of the people, even many of Ephraim and Manasseh, Issachar and Zebulun, had not cleansed themselves, yet did they eat the Passover otherwise than it is written. For Hezekiah had prayed for them, saying, The good Yahweh pardon everyone who sets his heart to seek God, Yahweh, the God of his fathers, though not cleansed according to the purification of the sanctuary. Yahweh listened to Hezekiah, and healed the people (2 Chronicles 30:13-20).

This is the lesson of the New Covenant. Judah and some of Israel wanted to keep Passover, but they had not had time after their repentance to follow all of God's instructions. In that, they had sinned. In spite of their shortcomings, good Yahweh pardoned everyone who had set his heart to seek God. They could not deliberately ignore His instructions, but when they tried to obey Him and fell short, He pardoned them:

> The children of Israel who were present at Jerusalem kept the feast of unleavened bread seven days with great gladness; and the Levites and the priests praised Yahweh day by day, singing with loud instruments to Yahweh. Hezekiah spoke comfortably to all the Levites who had good understanding in the service of Yahweh. So they ate throughout the feast for the seven days, offering sacrifices of peace offerings, and making confession to Yahweh, the God of their fathers. The whole assembly took counsel to keep other seven days; and they kept other seven days with gladness....
>
> All the assembly of Judah, with the priests and the Levites, and all the assembly who came out of Israel, and the foreigners who came out of the land of Israel, and who lived in Judah, rejoiced. So there was great joy in Jerusalem; for since the time of Solomon the son of David king of Israel there was not the like in Jerusalem. Then the priests the Levites arose and blessed the people: and their voice was heard, and their prayer came up to his holy habitation, even to heaven (2 Chronicles 30:21-23, 25-27).

This was quite a marvelous revival at that feast of Unleavened Bread. Those people took the time to make the trip and fellowship with Yahweh. Was that wasted time? *"Their voice was heard, and their prayer came up to his holy habitation, even to heaven."* Those who refused to keep the feasts thought that they were a waste of time. But when you don't spend time with God, you wind up with a wasted life.

Hezekiah's son Manasseh led Judah back into evil, as did his grandson Amon. Then Hezekiah's great-grandson Josiah turned the kingdom back to God:

> Josiah was eight years old when he began to reign; and he reigned thirty-one years in Jerusalem. He did that which

was right in the eyes of Yahweh, and walked in the ways of David his father, and didn't turn aside to the right hand or to the left. For in the eighth year of his reign, while he was yet young, [when he was sixteen years old] he began to seek after the God of David his father; and in the twelfth year [when he was twenty years old], he began to purge Judah and Jerusalem from the high places, and the Asherim, and the engraved images, and the molten images (2 Chronicles 34:1-3).

What happened to Josiah between ages sixteen and twenty?

At age sixteen he began to seek after the God of David, his ancient ancestor. This was among people who mostly ignored that God. The Temple was not being used, the priesthood wasn't functioning, and the feasts were forgotten.

At age sixteen Josiah began to seek God, and at age twenty he began to attack idolatry.

What happened to Josiah between ages sixteen and twenty? "But from there you shall seek Yahweh your God, and you shall find him, when you search after him with all your heart and with all your soul" (Deuteronomy 4:29). "I love those who love me. Those who seek me diligently will find me" (Proverbs 8:17).

When Josiah sought God, he found Him. When Josiah found Him, then Josiah's spirit was stirred into action. He didn't just get platitudes. He got an attitude:

They broke down the altars of the Baals in his presence; and the incense altars that were on high above them he cut down; and the Asherim, and the engraved images, and the molten images, he broke in pieces, and made dust of them, and strewed it on the graves of those who had sacrificed to them. He burnt the bones of the priests on their altars, and purged Judah and Jerusalem. So did he in the cities of Manasseh and Ephraim and Simeon, even to Naphtali, around in their ruins. He broke down the altars, and beat the Asherim and the engraved images into powder, and cut down all the incense altars throughout all the land of Israel, and returned to Jerusalem. Now in the eighteenth year of his reign [when he was twenty-six years old], when he had purged the land and the house, he sent

> Shaphan the son of Azaliah, and Maaseiah the governor of
> the city, and Joah the son of Joahaz the recorder, to repair
> the house of Yahweh his God (2 Chronicles 34:4-8).

Josiah had reigned for eighteen years. In a human life, that's a
long time. He had destroyed the idols, but he had not yet
reinstituted the Temple worship. Josiah had not learned about
God from his father. Some of the basics he had to learn for
himself. Look at what they found when they got into the
Temple, which even the priests had forgotten:

> They came to Hilkiah the high priest, and delivered the
> money that was brought into the house of God, which
> the Levites, the keepers of the threshold, had gathered of
> the hand of Manasseh and Ephraim, and of all the
> remnant of Israel, and of all Judah and Benjamin, and of
> the inhabitants of Jerusalem. They delivered it into the
> hand of the workmen who had the oversight of the
> house of Yahweh; and the workmen who labored in the
> house of Yahweh gave it to mend and repair the house;
> even to the carpenters and to the builders gave they it, to
> buy cut stone, and timber for couplings, and to make
> beams for the houses which the kings of Judah had
> destroyed. The men did the work faithfully: and the
> overseers of them were Jahath and Obadiah, the Levites,
> of the sons of Merari; and Zechariah and Meshullam, of
> the sons of the Kohathites, to set it forward; and others of
> the Levites, all who were skillful with instruments of
> music. Also they were over the bearers of burdens, and
> set forward all who did the work in every manner of
> service: and of the Levites there were scribes, and
> officers, and porters. When they brought out the money
> that was brought into the house of Yahweh, Hilkiah the
> priest found the book of the law of Yahweh given by
> Moses. Hilkiah answered Shaphan the scribe, I have
> found the book of the law in the house of Yahweh.
> Hilkiah delivered the book to Shaphan. Shaphan carried
> the book to the king, and moreover brought back word
> to the king, saying, All that was committed to your
> servants, they are doing. They have emptied out the
> money that was found in the house of Yahweh, and have
> delivered it into the hand of the overseers, and into the

hand of the workmen. Shaphan the scribe told the king, saying, Hilkiah the priest has delivered me a book (2 Chronicles 34:9-18).

A book? *Hilkiah the priest has delivered me a book.*

Excuse me—*A BOOK*?

Not just a book, but the Book. This was the mind of God written down. Josiah had done all that he had been doing without the Guidebook: "Your word is a lamp to my feet, and a light for my path" (Psalms 119:105).

When they found the Book, the first thing they did was read it to the king. "Shaphan read therein before the king. It happened, when the king had heard the words of the law, that he tore his clothes" (2 Chronicles 34:18-19). Softhearted King Josiah did all that he could to serve Yahweh. Then he heard the *Torah*, and tore his clothes. He tore his clothes when he heard the *Torah*—because of all that he had not been doing, because he had not known:

> The king commanded Hilkiah, and Ahikam the son of Shaphan, and Abdon the son of Micah, and Shaphan the scribe, and Asaiah the king's servant, saying, Go inquire of Yahweh for me, and for those who are left in Israel and in Judah, concerning the words of the book that is found; for great is the wrath of Yahweh that is poured out on us, because our fathers have not kept the word of Yahweh, to do according to all that is written in this book. So Hilkiah, and they whom the king had commanded, went to Huldah the prophetess, the wife of Shallum the son of Tokhath, the son of Hasrah, keeper of the wardrobe (now she lived in Jerusalem in the second quarter); and they spoke to her to that effect. She said to them, Thus says Yahweh, the God of Israel: Tell the man who sent you to me, Thus says Yahweh, Behold, I will bring evil on this place, and on its inhabitants, even all the curses that are written in the book which they have read before the king of Judah. Because they have forsaken me, and have burned incense to other gods, that they might provoke me to anger with all the works of their hands; therefore is my wrath poured out on this place, and it shall not be quenched. But to the king of Judah, who sent you to inquire of Yahweh, thus you shall tell him, Thus says Yahweh, the God of Israel: As touching the words which you have heard, because your

heart was tender, and you humbled yourself before God, when you heard his words against this place, and against its inhabitants, and have humbled yourself before me, and have torn your clothes, and wept before me; I also have heard you, says Yahweh. Behold, I will gather you to your fathers, and you shall be gathered to your grave in peace, neither shall your eyes see all the evil that I will bring on this place, and on its inhabitants. They brought back word to the king. Then the king sent and gathered together all the elders of Judah and Jerusalem. The king went up to the house of Yahweh, and all the men of Judah and the inhabitants of Jerusalem, and the priests, and the Levites, and all the people, both great and small: and he read in their ears all the words of the book of the covenant that was found in the house of Yahweh. The king stood in his place, and made a covenant before Yahweh, to walk after Yahweh, and to keep his commandments, and his testimonies, and his statutes, with all his heart, and with all his soul, to perform the words of the covenant that were written in this book. He caused all who were found in Jerusalem and Benjamin to stand to it. The inhabitants of Jerusalem did according to the covenant of God, the God of their fathers. Josiah took away all the abominations out of all the countries that pertained to the children of Israel, and made all who were found in Israel to serve, even to serve Yahweh their God. All his days they didn't depart from following Yahweh, the God of their fathers (2 Chronicles 34: 20-33).

That was Josiah. What a record, to be preserved for all time! Oh, yes—and Josiah immediately had Judah keep a festival:

Josiah kept a Passover to Yahweh in Jerusalem: and they killed the Passover on the fourteenth day of the first month....

The children of Israel who were present kept the Passover at that time, and the feast of unleavened bread seven days. There was no Passover like that kept in Israel from the days of Samuel the prophet; neither did any of the kings of Israel keep such a Passover as Josiah kept, and the priests, and the Levites, and all Judah and Israel who were present, and the inhabitants of Jerusalem. In the eighteenth year of the reign of Josiah was this Passover kept (2 Chronicles 35:1, 17-19).

The year that they found the book of the law, Josiah kept the feasts. Unlike the Roman feasts, Yahweh's feasts are not a time to throw up. They're a time to look up:

> As the deer pants for the water brooks, so my soul pants after you, God. My soul thirsts for God, for the living God. When shall I come and appear before God? My tears have been my food day and night, while they continually ask me, "Where is your God?" These things I remember, and pour out my soul within me, how I used to go with the crowd, and led them to the house of God, with the voice of joy and praise, a multitude *keeping a holy day* (Psalms 42:1-4).

They are a spiritual spring in a parched desert.

In sum, Israel was to take time for God's festivals three times a year, nineteen festival days, which took up about a whole month of their year. Those people who thought more of gold than they did of God always quit keeping those festivals. To somebody trying to get ahead, the feasts seemed just a waste of time.

CHAPTER 8

HEY—TAKE THE YEAR OFF!

God had Israel take off the seventh day of every week and about a month off for annual festivals.

Isn't that enough?

No.

How about a year off?

How about two years off in a row? "For six years you shall sow your land, and shall gather in its increase, but the seventh year you shall let it rest and lie fallow, that the poor of your people may eat; and what they leave the animal of the field shall eat. In like manner you shall deal with your vineyard and with your olive grove" (Exodus 23:10-11).

Six years they were to sow their land, but the seventh they were not to plant it. The land was to rest. That which grew of itself on the land the owner and the poor could eat. The grapes and olives that grew in the seventh year could be eaten, but they were not to be harvested by the owner:

> Yahweh said to Moses in Mount Sinai, "Speak to the children of Israel, and tell them, 'When you come into the land which I give you, then the land shall keep a Sabbath to Yahweh. Six years you shall sow your field, and six years you shall prune your vineyard, and gather in its fruits; but in the seventh year there shall be a Sabbath of solemn rest for the land, a Sabbath to Yahweh. You shall not sow your field or prune your vineyard. What grows of itself in your harvest you shall not reap, and the grapes of your undressed vine you shall not gather. It shall be a year

of solemn rest for the land. The Sabbath of the land shall
be for food for you; for yourself, for your servant, for your
maid, for your hired servant, and for your stranger, who
lives as a foreigner with you. For your livestock also, and
for the animals that are in your land, shall all its increase
be for food'" (Leviticus 25:1-7).

In the sabbath year they were not to sow or prune. They just
didn't farm. Since nearly all the people of the nation worked the
land, this meant that they took every seventh year off.

What?

They took every seventh year off.

So what were they to eat during the year that they didn't
farm?

> Therefore you shall do my statutes, and keep my
> ordinances and do them; and you shall dwell in the land
> in safety. The land shall yield its fruit, and you shall eat
> your fill, and dwell therein in safety. If you said, "What
> shall we eat the seventh year? Behold, we shall not sow,
> nor gather in our increase;" then I will command my
> blessing on you in the sixth year, and it shall bring forth
> fruit for the three years. You shall sow the eighth year,
> and eat of the fruits, the old store; until the ninth year,
> until its fruits come in, you shall eat the old store
> (Leviticus 25:18-22).

Just as God gave them enough manna on the sixth day to last
through the seventh, so He promised to give them enough
harvest in the sixth year to last through the seventh and on
until the harvest of the eighth year came in.

So every seventh year they took off from work—with pay.

Have you ever known anybody in your life who took
every seventh year off from work? Probably not.

If someone did take every seventh year off from work,
how would he be viewed today?

Lazy, worthless, no account, and most of all—not ambitious.

Yet to take every seventh year off was not the place of the
indolent, but the diligent—those most dedicated to God. Those

most lacking in dedication to God worked that seventh year. You see, it all depends on what you are trying to achieve in life.

The land sabbath freed them from the concerns of self— they had their year's provisions—so they could look beyond their selfish interests.

The land sabbath was also a form of sharing. Whatever the land grew of itself could be eaten by the owner, but since the owner already had all he could eat, the poor people and the animals could eat of that volunteer growth. The land owner was not to store away the produce of the seventh year. That would be selfish. He already had enough.

The land sabbath was a time of restoring for the land itself. The land lay fallow, uncultivated for a whole year, just resting. This was a time of restoration for God's creation. Not only did that allow nutrients in the soil to replenish, but when crops did not grow in the whole country, the pests and diseases which thrived on those crops had a rough year.

The sabbath year was a year's paid vacation, a time of sharing with the poor and the wild animals, a rest and restoring for the land, and a pestilence on pests and diseases.

I spoke with a Christian friend once about all the time that Israel took away from work. He thought that they weren't very productive. He thought that America today was called to be productive. America does work a lot today. But what is America producing today?

It produces a lot of stuff and gadgets. It also produces families, half of which self-destruct. It produces some of the world's highest rates of teen pregnancy, abortions, teen suicide, murder, and a number of other markers of destruction.

It's obvious from what we have seen with the Sabbath, the feasts, and the land sabbath that God didn't want His people dedicating their whole lives to stuff. He wanted them to dedicate a major part of their lives to Him.

But again—why should they dedicate their lives to just getting more stuff, or being productive? They had God's

rantee that they would have everything they needed, as
g as they had Him.

What a difference that could make in a person's life, if he just
has the confidence that God will give him everything he needs.

If you truly believed that God would supply all your
needs, that would loose your mind from worry.

It would free your time for prayer and study.

It would make you generous with others.

As the Philippians were with Paul:

> In my life in union with the Lord it is a great joy to me that
> after so long a time you once more had the chance of
> showing that you care for me. I don't mean that you had
> stopped caring for me—you just had no chance to show it.
> And I am not saying this because I feel neglected, for I
> have learned to be satisfied with what I have. I know what
> it is to be in need and what it is to have more than enough.
> I have learned this secret, so that anywhere, at any time, I
> am content, whether I am full or hungry, whether I have
> too much or too little. I have the strength to face all
> conditions by the power that Christ gives me. But it was
> very good of you to help me in my troubles. You
> Philippians know very well that when I left Macedonia in
> the early days of preaching the Good News, you were the
> only church to help me; you were the only ones who
> shared my profits and losses. More than once when I
> needed help in Thessalonica, you sent it to me. It is not
> that I just want to receive gifts; rather, I want to see profit
> added to your account. Here, then, is my receipt for
> everything you have given me—and it has been more than
> enough! I have all I need now that Epaphroditus has
> brought me all your gifts. They are like a sweet-smelling
> offering to God, a sacrifice which is acceptable and
> pleasing to him. And with all his abundant wealth
> through Christ Jesus, my God will supply all your needs.
> To our God and Father be the glory forever and ever!
> Amen (Philippians 4:10-20, GNB).

Notice a key point here. *With all his abundant wealth through
Christ Jesus, my God will supply all your needs.* That sounds a lot
like the manna guarantee that Yahweh gave to Israel in the

wilderness. Hey, God will supply all your needs. Your manna will be there in the morning. So if you have enough, and know you always will, you won't waste your life trying to get more, and you will be willing to freely share what you have. After all, you have enough!

It's not surprising, then, that during the Sabbath year, Yahweh had the Israelites cancel any loans they had made to their brothers.

That's right. Loans canceled. Bad debts made for good deeds by those who forgave them:

> At the end of every seven years you shall make a release. This is the manner of the release: every creditor shall release that which he has lent to his neighbor; he shall not exact it of his neighbor and his brother; because Yahweh's release has been proclaimed. Of a foreigner you may exact it: but whatever of yours is with your brother your hand shall release. However there shall be no poor with you; (for Yahweh will surely bless you in the land which Yahweh your God gives you for an inheritance to possess it); if only you diligently listen to the voice of Yahweh your God, to observe to do all this commandment which I command you this day (Deuteronomy 15:1-5).

Let's read that again in the Contemporary English Version:

> Every seven years you must announce, "The LORD says loans do not need to be paid back." Then if you have loaned money to another Israelite, you can no longer ask for payment. This law applies only to loans you have made to other Israelites. Foreigners will still have to pay back what you have loaned them. No one in Israel should ever be poor. The LORD your God is giving you this land, and he has promised to make you very successful, if you obey his laws and teachings that I'm giving you today. You will lend money to many nations, but you won't have to borrow. You will rule many nations, but they won't rule you (Deuteronomy 15:1-5).

Are you shell-shocked by now at what God expected from Israel? All that time away from work, and then canceling unpaid loans?

What Yahweh asks of His people is the opposite of avarice. We might call it *have*arice. Since they have a guarantee to always have enough, they don't have to be greedy at all.

Their lives are fully consumed, not with consumption, but with giving. They give to God and to others.

With all his abundant wealth through Christ Jesus, my God will supply all your needs!

It's like zucchini in the summer.

We live in the country, where many people have a vegetable garden. Some veggies are harder to grow than others. Zucchini is easy to grow. A plant will put on a lot of zucchini, and each one can get very big.

Some veggies are more delicious than others. Some people don't consider any veggies delicious. Zucchini has its uses, but it is not often considered the most delicious vegetable.

Therefore, in our neck of the woods, in the middle of summer, when the gardens are in full production, you may be gifted with zucchini.

However, when we are gifted with zucchini, our usual response is, "Thanks ever so much, but we have enough."

That's what happens when everybody has zucchini. Everybody is generous, because everybody has enough. Paul said:

> I have coveted no man's silver or gold or apparel. Yea, you yourselves know that these hands have ministered to my needs, and to those who were with me. I have shown you all things, that working in this way we ought to help the weak, and to remember the words of the Lord Jesus, that He Himself said, It is more blessed to give than to receive (Acts 20:33-35, MKJV).

There's the law. It is more blessed to give than to receive. Giving is serving God by serving others, and it is believing

God. Since you believe He will take care of you, you can give to others:

> When you do good deeds, don't try to show off. If you do, you won't get a reward from your Father in heaven. When you give to the poor, don't blow a loud horn. That's what show-offs do in the meeting places and on the street corners, because they are always looking for praise. I can assure you that they already have their reward. When you give to the poor, don't let anyone know about it. Then your gift will be given in secret. Your Father knows what is done in secret, and he will reward you (Matthew 6:1-4, CEV).

When you give—and you don't do it to show off—your Father will reward you.

So the Israelites, with the "God guarantee," had to stop farming in the Sabbath year. For most of them, that stopped their income for that year. They also had to cancel any loans they had made to poor brothers.

Okay, then. If they had to forgive that loan, then at least they could charge enough interest on the loan to allow for all that risk. Right? No. "If you lend money to any of my people with you who is poor, you shall not be to him as a creditor; neither shall you charge him interest" (Exodus 22:25). No interest on the loan to the poor brother. In view of the above, I tell you what—I ain't going to make that loan at all.

In the great financial collapse of 2008, one of the great problems was that banks quit loaning funds to each other. After a few of the major banks got into major trouble—they ran out of money because they had made such bad loans—many other banks just quit loaning money. They didn't know who was good and who was bad, and whether or not they would get their money back. So they just stuck their money in their pockets and refused to get it out.

God warned Israel not to do that with a poor brother:

> If a poor man, one of your brothers, is with you within any of your gates in your land which Yahweh your God

gives you, you shall not harden your heart, nor shut your hand from your poor brother; but you shall surely open your hand to him, and shall surely lend him sufficient for his need in that which he wants. Beware that there not be a base thought in your heart, saying, The seventh year, the year of release, is at hand; and your eye be evil against your poor brother, and you give him nothing; and he cry to Yahweh against you, and it be sin to you. You shall surely give him, and your heart shall not be grieved when you give to him; because that for this thing Yahweh your God will bless you in all your work, and in all that you put your hand to. For the poor will never cease out of the land: therefore I command you, saying, You shall surely open your hand to your brother, to your needy, and to your poor, in your land (Deuteronomy 15, 7-11).

The *World English Bible* is based on the old American Standard Version, which translates basically word for word. Other translations—dynamic—try to translate the thought of the words. The Contemporary English Version in that passage says:

Be careful! Don't say to yourself, "Soon it will be the seventh year, and then I won't be able to get my money back." It would be horrible for you to think that way and to be so selfish that you refuse to help the poor. They are your relatives, and if you don't help them, they may ask the LORD to decide whether you have done wrong. And he will say that you are guilty. You should be happy to give the poor what they need, because then the LORD will make you successful in everything you do (Deuteronomy 15:9-10, CEV).

We must remember that if you love your neighbor as yourself, and you loan him money to feed and clothe his children, that is like doing that for yourself. *If* you love him as yourself.

You see, wise fiduciary policy would not make an unsecured loan to a poor person who had no good prospects of paying it back. Wise fiduciary policy would never make a loan for no interest. Wise fiduciary policy would not forgive a loan, just because the debtor couldn't pay it back.

The human's wise fiduciary policy is the opposite of fiduciary policy. God's banking regulations focus on givi ͜ getting. That's why God's wisdom so stuns the human mind. It's you backwards.

Christ said about the same thing as the Old Testament law: "And if anyone would sue you and take your tunic, let him have your cloak as well. And if anyone forces you to go one mile, go with him two miles. Give to the one who begs from you, and do not refuse the one who would borrow from you" (Matthew 5:40-42, ESV). God's way is the way of giving. The basis of giving is God. You give because you know He will give to you.

Greed is the opposite of God. Greed is the ultimate lack of faith. It is the attempt to establish oneself without God.

God told His people to take the Sabbath day off; to visit with Him on His festivals; to take a year off from work every seventh year; and to cancel any loans they had made to poor brothers, which, incidentally, they had to make.

Every seven years this agrarian economy had a systematic and expected wealth adjustment. The rich got poorer and the poor got richer, and everybody had enough. Debt did not build up, greed did not grow, and the boom-bust cycle was busted. That would not have been traumatic for the whole economy because it was expected, although some of the greedier accumulators who did not enjoy forgiving loans and taking a whole year off from work may have felt a wee bit of trauma.

CHAPTER 9

THE JUBILEE

For most, *once in every life* there came a Jubilee. The average life is about seventy years long:

> For a thousand years in your sight are just like yesterday when it is past, like a watch in the night. You sweep them away as they sleep. In the morning they sprout like new grass. In the morning it sprouts and springs up. By evening, it is withered and dry. For we are consumed in your anger. We are troubled in your wrath. You have set our iniquities before you, our secret sins in the light of your presence. For all our days have passed away in your wrath. We bring our years to an end as a sigh. The days of our years are seventy, or even by reason of strength eighty years; yet their pride is but labor and sorrow, for it passes quickly, and we fly away (Psalms 90:4-10).

A thousand years are to God as just a part of the night, but humans are stuck with seventy years. So about once in every life came a Jubilee, which occurred every fifty years.

There were some who were young when a Jubilee year came around, and they might see another Jubilee before they died. But they would really have been affected by only one Jubilee when they were working adults. A small number, who by reason of strength lived eight decades, would experience two Jubilees.

The word *jubilee*, or *jubile* in the old King James, is a derivative of the Hebrew word *yobel*, which *Strong's Concordance* says is the blast of a trumpet. *The International Standard Bible Encyclopedia* says: *"The Hebrew word* yobhel *stands for* ḳeren ha-yobhel, *meaning the horn of a ram. Now, such a horn can be made into a trumpet, and thus the word* yobhel *came to be used as a synonym of trumpet."*[1]

After seven sabbath years, or forty-nine years, on the Day of Atonement—a day of fasting and greatest humility—the blowing of the trumpet began the Jubilee year, or the *yobel* year:

> You shall count off seven Sabbaths of years, seven times seven years; and there shall be to you the days of seven Sabbaths of years, even forty-nine years. Then you shall sound the loud trumpet on the tenth day of the seventh month. On the Day of Atonement you shall sound the trumpet throughout all your land. You shall make the fiftieth year holy, and proclaim liberty throughout the land to all its inhabitants. It shall be a Jubilee to you; and each of you shall return to his own property, and each of you shall return to his family. That fiftieth year shall be a Jubilee to you. In it you shall not sow, neither reap that which grows of itself, nor gather from the undressed vines. For it is a Jubilee; it shall be holy to you. You shall eat of its increase out of the field. In this Year of Jubilee each of you shall return to his property. If you sell anything to your neighbor, or buy from your neighbor, you shall not wrong one another. According to the number of years after the Jubilee you shall buy from your neighbor. According to the number of years of the crops he shall sell to you. According to the length of the years you shall increase its price, and according to the shortness of the years you shall diminish its price; for he is selling the number of the crops to you. You shall not wrong one another; but you shall fear your God: for I am Yahweh your God. Therefore you shall do my statutes, and keep my ordinances and do them; and you shall dwell in the land in safety. The land shall yield its fruit, and you shall eat your fill, and dwell therein in safety (Leviticus 25:8-19).

The Jubilee year caused jubilation. It was the year of liberty. "Proclaim liberty throughout the land" is on the Liberty Bell in Philadelphia, Pennsylvania, to memorialize American independence from the English king.

What did the Jubilee year do?

It was a restoration.

ALL LAND RETURNED TO THE ORIGINAL FAMILY.

The Holy Land was not really owned by individual families, but they were allowed to use it. The Holy Land was Yahweh's land. He kicked the Canaanites out because they disobeyed Him and then He brought Israel in. When Israel disobeyed Him, He kicked them out of his Holy Land, too.

Property was to be bought and sold according to how many years were left in the Jubilee cycle. At the Jubilee, the land returned back to the original clan to whom God had given its use. If someone had not done well and had lost that land, the next generation of that family would receive a chance with the same family land.

The nation was not to become locked into a small number of families controlling all the land, as happened in England. Food is the bottom line of wealth. Food comes from the land. Therefore land is the basis of wealth. The common people of old England did not own land, could not get land, and were locked into a perpetual system of subservience to the lord of the estate where they worked.

But not so in Israel. Although one generation might fail in their use of the land, the next generation of the family got their chance with the same land—at the year of Jubilee. What a marvelous system compared to the feudalism of Europe.

SERVANTS WON FREEDOM AT THE JUBILEE.

"Proclaim liberty!" meant that those who had been sold into servitude were freed. No Hebrew was to live in servitude longer than seven years, just as in colonial America, when servants indentured themselves for seven years to get passage to the New World. Regardless of how many years they had served, all Israelites gained freedom at the Jubilee.

KILLERS OBTAINED PARDON AT THE JUBILEE.

Murderers were to be stoned. However, sometimes people die at the hand of others who did not intend to kill them; we would call that manslaughter or negligent homicide. Someone who killed another by accident could flee to one of the cities of refuge established for them. If the killer made it to the city of refuge, then he could live in that city and receive mercy for his crime of negligence. If he left that city, then the victim's family could kill the killer for his crime. On the year of Jubilee, these killers received forgiveness and freedom. They could freely leave the city of refuge where they had in effect been prisoners, and enjoy liberty through all the land.

Also, on the Jubilee year, as on the sabbath year, farmers did not sow or harvest crops. That made for two sabbath years in a row, years forty-nine and fifty, without working the farmland.

In sum, once the Jubilee year arrived, nobody in the land remained in bondage.

Those under any sort of oppression—whether of their land, their service, or in prison—received release. Those not under some type of oppression remained free, of course. Jubilee was a year of liberty for all.

How would you have reacted to the Jubilee?

When Israel first entered the Holy Land, each family was given land to use in perpetuity. They owed no debt and they paid no taxes. Each family made their living from their own land and their own labor.

Over time, some did well and some did poorly. Those who did poorly did so because of their disobedience to God and His laws. The poorest of the poor then sold their land or sold their lives and labor to become the servants of those who had done well.

Actually, Israelites should never have gotten so poor that they had to sell their land and their lives. First, they should have obeyed God and then would have received His blessing. Second, their brethren should have aided them and helped them not get to such a desperate plight.

When a man ran into hardship, first he would have sold his land. This almost doomed him to stay poor or become still poorer, because he had lost his means to generate wealth. When a man sold his land, since the land was his prime means of generating wealth, he had great difficulty getting enough money to buy the land back.

Now he could only earn from his labor. However, as he labored for someone else, that party also profited from the poor person's labor. The laborer only got a share of the profits he earned from working the other man's land.

Some who had sold their land would see their own mistakes and change. Others would persist in the same habits that had gotten them in trouble in the first place and would become still poorer. They would then have to sell themselves into servitude just to stay alive.

Time would sort the efficient from the less efficient. The efficient would employ by the less efficient. The well-to-do would earn from:

1. His labor;

2. His land;

3. The poor family's labor;

4. The poor family's land.

The poor man was barely able to stay alive.

This effect would be compounded with more time and property, allowing the one who already had more than enough to accumulate still more. This is similar to a game of checkers. At the start of the game, both players begin with twelve men and no kings. As the game progresses, one player will wind up with more kings and men than the other player. When that happens, it is then easier for the player with more kings and men to capture still more of the checkers of the one with fewer.

In most societies, this momentum grows until finally a relative few control most of the wealth. This wealth then passes from generation to generation, often increasing with each generation. Sometimes a rich family will fall, and sometimes a poor family will rise. Generally, however, the rich get richer and the poor get poorer, unless something interrupts that process.

The Jubilee cycle was unlike anything else ever set up. The poor were helped by interest-free loans, which were totally forgiven if they were unpaid by the sabbath year. The poor could glean behind the reapers of their more successful neighbors. They received help from the poor tithe. During the sabbath year the poor could eat from the crops which grew voluntarily.

Then, in the fiftieth year, just when the accumulating process in a normal society would really be gathering momentum and wealth would be getting quite unbalanced, those families who had lost their land and had lost their liberty were restored to their original estate, both of land and freedom.

"Proclaim liberty throughout all the land unto all the inhabitants thereof."

At that point, all Israel was free. None were in bondage. Every family had its land, just as at the beginning. Every person had his freedom.

How would such a system affect the attitude of those who lived under it?

Imagine a young man twenty-one years old at the year of Jubilee, from a poor family. They had lost their land, and for several years he had worked as a servant of a neighbor. At the blowing of the trumpet on Yom Kippur, the day of covering, the Jubilee year began.

The young man was now a free man. His family regained their land and he got to work it. His years as a servant made him determined not to repeat that fate. When he had worked as a servant, he did what his master wanted. He did not live where he wanted to live, but had to live where the master wanted. He lived in constant fear of displeasing the master.

As a free man, he could work for himself. He could make his own plans, build his own business, and live where he wanted, on his own land.

The young man worked hard. When he had worked for the master, the days were too long. When he worked for himself, the days were too short. He made a good living for himself and his own young family. His barns filled up. He even began to accumulate extra.

After some years, he used his extra wealth to buy the use of the land of someone who had not done well. Of course, he could have used his extra wealth to help the neighbor back on his feet, maybe by making an interest-free loan which he would forgive at the Sabbath year, but he chose to use his extra wealth to expand his own business.

Now the young man was able to gain from two properties, his and his neighbor's. That meant more of his time taken up with work. He didn't really need the extra gain, because he already had enough, but he chose to try to get more.

The poor neighbor who had no land soon became worse off and had to also sell himself into servitude to our young man, just to stay alive. This extra labor served to bring the young man still more profit.

Through the years, our industrious Israelite expanded his little empire, by taking advantage of poor brothers. The more he got, the more he was able to get.

His domain grew until he had much land and many animals and a large staff of servant employees to help run his growing business. Actually, they did most of the hard work in the business, getting all the gain for him and none for them. He told them where to live, what to do, and how to do it.

The bigger his holdings got, the more time and attention they took. In actuality, he did not eat more than he had when he was poorer. There was only so much that he would eat, after all. His clothes were certainly finer, but they covered his body and kept him warm the same as his clothes had always done.

To pay for getting more, the young man traded his life. His life was consumed in this way until he was not a young man any more. He had gathered much, and he had spent much to gather it. The figures in his tally had grown, while the years of his life had flown.

Finally he hit his seventieth year. Or rather, it hit him. His health had slipped away from the toll of the years and the toil of his life. His family was fragmented. Families are funny. Like a business, they take time. If they don't get time, they're not family.

But the septuagenarian felt satisfied with his life. He had gone from a servant to a master and was pleased with all that he had accumulated—the lands, the servants, the enormous empire that was his.

He felt as if his life meant something, and he could actually see that worth. He could visually measure the result of his life, the lands, the servants, the bulging barns. One of his few regrets was that a few others had accumulated even more than he had. If only he had had more time.

As he entered his seventieth year, he was rich, honored and dying. And then…

Jubilee!

Release! Liberty to the inhabitants of the land!

Suddenly, with the sound of a trumpet, his empire was gone.

All the extra land he had farmed went back to the original families. All his servants were freed from their bondage to him, and they gleefully rushed away to work for themselves on their own lands.

The point of this example?

This guy's life was pointless.

He worked fifty years only to see the fruits of his life vanish. He traded his life to get more than he needed. The sum total of his life was that he had more than enough, and that disappeared at the Jubilee. This man had spent his life breaking the natural law to love God more than himself and to love others as himself. Like Cain, he was not his brother's keeper. He looked out for himself.

Would you have done that? If you had lived under the Jubilee system, would you have worked your whole adult life to build an empire that would be blown away with the blast of the ram's horn?

Surely not.

You would see the futility of it all. You would not cash in your life, your wife, your children, your health for something that you would have to give back. You would know that at the Jubilee, your excess wealth would be redistributed, undoing on the Day of Atonement most of what you had accumulated. Just as the Israelites stopped collecting extra manna only to have it rot, so you would stop wasting your life collecting more than enough, knowing that at the end of your life it would do you just as much good as rotten manna.

The Jubilee system would have changed the whole society. There would have been no catastrophic debt-detonated depressions. Any economic adjustment would have been orderly and expected. The Jubilee system would have also changed the individual. It would have discouraged you from dedicating your life to amassing wealth, when you knew it would all pass on when the trumpet blew.

CHAPTER 10

THE WHOLE JUBILEE SYSTEM

That's the Jubilee system, the way God set it up when He brought Israel, His chosen people, into Israel, His Holy Land.

Israelites had free land, no debt, and no taxes. They were guaranteed abundant crops if they obeyed God. Since they had enough and didn't need more, they could spend a major part of their lives fulfilling the natural law to love God and others.

Every Sabbath day they were freed from work and self-gratification.

Three times a year they worshiped Yahweh at His feasts.

Every seventh year they received a year off from work, with pay. All loans were canceled.

Every fiftieth year lost liberty was restored. Servants were released, killers were let out of prison cities, and all land went from the accumulators back to the original families.

In this amazing system, unlike anything else ever known in human history, there was no place for greed or usurious debt. This cycle, which was contrary to greed and debt, had about the same frequency as the Kondratieff Wave, which functions on greed and debt.

In an article cited in the first chapter of this book, from October 13, 2008, Joseph Farah of WorldNetDaily went on to comment on the debt problem:

> The answer is found in Leviticus 25. It's called the year of jubilee. It is a system of forgiveness of debts that occurred in ancient Israel every fifty years. And, ironically, it just so

happens a new year of jubilee began last week on Yom Kippur, or the Day of Atonement—the highest holy day in the Hebrew calendar.[1]

Earlier we talked about the proverb that says that the borrower is servant to the lender. Most people buy their homes with a mortgage and then pay on that mortgage for decades. Actually, often the homeowner does not pay off his mortgage, but trades up to a bigger house with a bigger mortgage, maintaining his indebtedness almost continually.

Most people consider it a great benefit to be able to buy a home with a mortgage. Is God's proverb true, then? When a person takes on a mortgage for his home, is he indeed a servant to the lender?

He is, in this way. His life is controlled by that payment. In that debt situation, there is little possibility that he could live like an Israelite, and be able to take time out to spend with God, as God instructed.

This has become so much the norm that it is thought wholly abnormal to do otherwise. Our lives are controlled by payments. We consider this a blessing, because we are able to have homes and cars and appliances and electronics and clothes much sooner and in greater quantity than we would if we did not carry debt. The big tradeoff that we make is control of our lives. We have to go to work every week, on whatever days of the week, all year, every year. God does not rule the time of our lives. Debt rules.

Stress from debt is often a major health factor. People with high levels of debt are much more likely to suffer health problems. Those problems include not just headaches and upset stomachs, but more serious problems. An Associated Press poll in 2008 found that people reporting high debt stress were much more likely to have ulcers, migraines, anxiety, depression, and even heart attacks.[2]

Debt can control where you live, how much you work, and, ultimately, who you are as an individual. If you spend almost all your life working just to keep up with your bills, how does that shape you as an individual? What would you be like if you didn't have to do that?

Debt plagued even so prominent a person as Thomas Jefferson. In 1787 he wrote to a friend, "The torment of mind I endure till the moment shall arrive when I shall not owe a shilling on earth is such really as to render life of little value." Jefferson never ever got out of debt. He died with a debt of $107,000, equal to a couple million dollars today.[3]

What a statement he made! He, who was involved in the establishment of a new nation which was to become the leader of the world, said that his life had little value because of his debt.

Debt devalues life. Debt changes who you are. Debt robs you of your God time.

God set Israel up the way He did primarily so they could spend time with Him and serve Him. Every seven years the debt burden was relieved, and every fifty years a major adjustment in economic wealth occurred with the land restoration.

America is now facing an economic adjustment:

> For years, Americans have been mocked for their materialistic nature. A "gotta have it now" mentality has become the norm for consumers, and the middle class has literally disguised itself as part of the wealthy. At nearly every level of our society, individuals have been living well beyond their means, thanks to a dirty four-letter word: debt.
>
> Behind the expensive cars, luxury clothing, hottest gadgets, and, of course, the McMansion homes, lies an enormous pile of debt. As a nation, we collectively have about $850 billion, or $9,659 per household, outstanding in credit card debt alone. Total U.S. household debt as a percentage of GDP has risen from 23.5% in 1952 to 97.8% today. The personal savings rate has been hovering in the 0-2% range for years. Putting money away for a rainy day has become a concept of yesteryear.
>
> But that rainy day is here.
>
> And it has made one heck of a grand, torrential entrance. Banks have collapsed, home "owners" have been forced

into foreclosure, and consumer confidence is at its lowest
level ever recorded[4]

What a coincidence that capitalist economies have an economic
rebalancing—debt busting—about every fifty years. This
economic adjustment, though, unlike the Jubilee system, is
often cataclysmic and traumatic.

In 2008, the financial collapse was quick and wide. People
saw much of their wealth evaporate within weeks, even days.
People study these economic cycles to try to ride the boom and
avoid the bust. They are constantly trying to figure out where
we are in the current cycle and where do we go from here—to
try to profit from that insight.

In doing so, they completely miss the main lesson of the
long wave.

In the Jubilee system, the big factor was the lack of
emphasis on wealth, and the enormous emphasis on God. *That
is the great lesson from the long wave cycle.* Don't waste your life
on wealth. It comes. It goes. God is eternal. Go with Him.
Notice this consistent teaching throughout the Bible:

> There is nothing better for a person than that he should eat
> and drink and find enjoyment in his toil. This also, I saw, is
> from the hand of God, for apart from him who can eat or
> who can have enjoyment? For to the one who pleases him
> God has given wisdom and knowledge and joy, but to the
> sinner he has given the business of gathering and collecting,
> only to give to one who pleases God. This also is vanity and
> a striving after wind (Ecclesiastes 2:24-26, ESV).

The sinner makes it his business to gather and collect. The Christ
follower makes it his business to gather wisdom from God.

> Jesus, seeing that he had become sad, said, "How difficult
> it is for those who have wealth to enter the kingdom of
> God! For it is easier for a camel to go through the eye of a
> needle than for a rich person to enter the kingdom of
> God" (Luke 18:24-25, ESV).

Preachers often explain away this statement of Christ. They do that to appease the rich people in their congregations. Note the obvious: camels do not fit through needle eyes, no matter how a preacher may explain it:

> Now there is great gain in godliness with contentment, for we brought nothing into the world, and we cannot take anything out of the world. But if we have food and clothing, with these we will be content. But those who desire to be rich fall into temptation, into a snare, into many senseless and harmful desires that plunge people into ruin and destruction. For the love of money is a root of all kinds of evils. It is through this craving that some have wandered away from the faith and pierced themselves with many pangs (1 Timothy 6:6-10, ESV).

If we have food and clothing—enough—*with these we will be content.* The love of money brings evil. It robs you of your life. "Keep your life free from love of money, and be content with what you have, for he has said, 'I will never leave you nor forsake you'" (Hebrews 13:5, ESV).

You have to work in order to live. But don't live just so you can work. If you are with God, He will never leave you nor forsake you, so you don't need anything else. Don't make the accumulation of wealth the focus of your life:

> Come now, you rich, weep and howl for the miseries that are coming upon you. Your riches have rotted and your garments are moth-eaten. Your gold and silver have corroded, and their corrosion will be evidence against you and will eat your flesh like fire. You have laid up treasure in the last days. Behold, the wages of the laborers who mowed your fields, which you kept back by fraud, are crying out against you, and the cries of the harvesters have reached the ears of the Lord of hosts. You have lived on the earth in luxury and in self-indulgence. You have fattened your hearts in a day of slaughter (James 5:1-5, ESV).

James was the brother of Y'shua and he sounded like it, in condemning a life focused on wealth.

Israel did have to work. God commanded them to work six days a week, and rest on the seventh. He commanded them to keep the feasts for about a month and work the rest of the year. He commanded them to take the sabbath year off and work the other six. God wanted them to accumulate enough to live on, but not to make accumulation the goal of their lives. They took these breaks from working to work on the really important things in life.

The Jubilee system repeated the lesson of the giving of the manna, where everybody had enough, nobody had too little, and nobody had too much. They did not have to center their lives around manna. Because they knew they would always have enough, they could center their lives around God.

That's the same lesson in the land sabbath. During that year when Israel was not to sow or reap, what would they do? They could do something to make money on the side, to try to get around the purpose of the sabbath year and try to "get ahead." Or, since they did not need to accumulate more since they would always have enough, they could use that year to serve God and others. Their hearts would determine their choice.

To accumulate wealth is to serve the self. Even people who have worked constantly for forty years and retire still usually focus on serving themselves. They are finally free of the burdens of making a living and paying off debts. Although little of their lives remain, what will they do with such life as they have? They have this big decision: what will they do with the little time they have left?

That's similar to the decision an Israelite had in the sabbath year: a whole year off from work—what to do, what to do?

What do almost all retirees do?

Not much of any lasting value. Some do. Some spend their last years actively trying to serve others. I know of a group of retirees who travel around helping to build church youth camps and such. Terrific.

But most don't.

Often they live in retirement communities, where the meaning of their lives is wrapped up in playing golf or bridge and involvement in a social circle with other old people who also don't know why they're alive. The highways are full of retirees who buy motor homes and putter around the country, aimlessly wandering from place to place, hardly connected with family, constantly looking for some new thing to whip up a little interest in their fading existence.

The only real purpose for life is to serve God and others:

> And he said to him, "You shall love the Lord your God with all your heart and with all your soul and with all your mind. This is the great and first commandment. And a second is like it: You shall love your neighbor as yourself. On these two commandments depend all the Law and the Prophets" (Matthew 22:37-40, ESV).

That's it. That's everything. That's your purpose.

> Blessed are the poor in spirit, for theirs is the kingdom of heaven. Blessed are those who mourn, for they shall be comforted. Blessed are the meek, for they shall inherit the earth. Blessed are those who hunger and thirst for righteousness, for they shall be satisfied. Blessed are the merciful, for they shall receive mercy. Blessed are the pure in heart, for they shall see God. Blessed are the peacemakers, for they shall be called sons of God. Blessed are those who are persecuted for righteousness' sake, for theirs is the kingdom of heaven. Blessed are you when others revile you and persecute you and utter all kinds of evil against you falsely on my account (Matthew 5:3-11, ESV).

Look at that—none of those things are self-seeking. Poor in spirit, mourn, meek, hunger for righteousness, merciful, pure, peacemakers, persecuted—none of those things serve the self. They all serve God and others.

Y'shua said that those who follow him forsake the self. "Then Jesus told his disciples, 'If anyone would come after me, let him deny himself and take up his cross and follow me'"

(Matthew 16:24, ESV). The Kondratieff Wave shows the futility of making wealth the focus of life. All these booms are followed by busts. So the wise person tries to figure out how to get in on the boom and miss the bust, right?

Wrong.

The wise person sees that the whole perpetual human cycle of greed and debt is not the way to live a life. You see, the Jubilee cycle or the long wave is a picture of a person's life. It's a picture of your life.

In your life, when you are young you have your boom years. Times are good. You can run, you can work, you can hear, you can see. Your innards work well. It seems as if this will never change.

But it does. The boom is always followed by the bust.

When I was young, I could run fast and throw hard. Several years ago, we had a school picnic for our little Christian school. We held a race between my fifteen-year-old daughter and her friend. I was about fifty at the time but didn't feel my age, so I wanted to join in the race with them. I was curious to see how far I had slid in athleticism. I did have the wisdom not to challenge the boys. But I thought that surely I could run with these teen girls!

We ran the race. "They're off!"

Well, they were off and I was awful. My daughter came in first. Her friend came in second. I brought up the rear, as the saying is, and with me, that had a more literal meaning.

In my defense, I will say that I did finish the forty-yard race.

The head of the school, who was about my age and also recalled the days when he ran and his feet actually moved, then challenged me to a race. Notice that he did not challenge my daughter or her friend, who came in ahead of me. No, he challenged me—Mr. Third Place—to a race.

Now where's the glory in that? If a race is run, the next guy should challenge the winner—not the guy who huffs in last place.

He insisted.

The school picnic was now charged with expectation. And with giggles. Who would win the race? Who would finish the race? Who would fall on his face in the race?

We raced!

Some time later… (as the Bible says, "in the process of time …") I won, about one step ahead of the other old fogey. It turned out his boom was slightly more busted than mine. Like me, his boom had lost its zoom.

> Young people, enjoy your youth. Be happy while you are still young. Do what you want to do, and follow your heart's desire. But remember that God is going to judge you for whatever you do. Don't let anything worry you or cause you pain. You aren't going to be young very long (Ecclesiastes 11:9-10, GNB).

The Jubilee cycle is like your life. You aren't going to be young very long. You have your boom years physically, and then you hit the big bear market:

> So remember your Creator while you are still young, before those dismal days and years come when you will say, "I don't enjoy life." That is when the light of the sun, the moon, and the stars will grow dim for you, and the rain clouds will never pass away. Then your arms, that have protected you, will tremble, and your legs, now strong, will grow weak. Your teeth will be too few to chew your food, and your eyes too dim to see clearly. Your ears will be deaf to the noise of the street. You will barely be able to hear the mill as it grinds or music as it plays, but even the song of a bird will wake you from sleep. You will be afraid of high places, and walking will be dangerous. Your hair will turn white; you will hardly be able to drag yourself along, and all desire will be gone. We are going to our final resting place, and then there will be mourning in the streets. The silver chain will snap, and the golden lamp will fall and break; the rope at the well will break, and the water jar will be shattered. Our bodies will return to the dust of the earth, and the breath of life will go back to God, who gave it to us (Ecclesiastes 12:1-7, GNB).

ember the example of our young man?

He worked fifty years only to see the fruits of his life vanish. He traded his life to get more than he needed. The sum total of his life was that he had more than enough, and that disappeared at the Jubilee. This man had spent his life breaking the natural law to love God more than himself and to love others as himself. Like Cain, he was not his brother's keeper. He looked out for himself.

Would you have done that? If you had lived under the Jubilee system, would you have worked your whole adult life to build an empire that would be blown away with the blast of the ram's horn?

Surely not.

You would see the futility of it all. You would not cash in your life, your wife, your children, your health for something that you would have to give back anyway. You would know that at the Jubilee, your excess wealth would be redistributed, undoing on the Day of Atonement most of what you had accumulated. Just as the Israelites stopped collecting extra manna only to have it rot, so you would stop wasting your life collecting more than enough, knowing that at the end of your life it would do you just as much good as rotten manna.

The Jubilee cycle is a picture of your life. Most people live as this man lived. They get instead of give. The Jubilee arrives for them at the end of life, when their final trumpet sounds, when all they have worked for passes on as they pass on. Most people spend their lives collecting excess manna, whose value rots on the day they die.

At the end of your life, when your bull market has turned bearish, you will want your riches to be stored beyond the cycles of human nature.

It is said that time is money. Time is love.

It is absolutely stunning to see how much God wanted from the people of Israel. He did not ask for great wealth to be given to him. All the wealth is His, anyway. He did not ask for human sacrifice. The pagan religions around the world, from the Canaanites in the Holy Land to the Indians in the Americas, demanded human sacrifice. Yahweh did not.

What He does want is love.

If you give love, you will give time. Love is time.

"You hang up first."

Young couples in love can't stay apart. Before my wife and I were married, when we were in college, we loved to be together. In one sense, our meetings weren't romantic at all. We would just meet on campus, surrounded by hundreds of other students, and engage in trivial conversation certainly very uninteresting to everyone else around us.

"How did speech class go?"

"Traumatic. How was American Lit?"

But to us it was magic. We were in love and together. Most of the time we didn't really do anything special together. Being together was special. What we did together didn't matter much. What did matter was that we were together. We just loved to spend time together.

What did we do when we weren't together? We talked on the phone with each other. What about?

"How did American Lit class go?"

"Traumatic. How was speech?"

How can two people spend so much time together, not doing much of anything, not even talking about much of anything? To do that with anyone else would be painfully boring, but with the one you love, it's painful *not* to be doing it.

Even hanging up the phone on a trivial conversation was difficult. Really!

"You hang up first."

"No, I can't. You hang up first."

Isn't that silly?

Not for people who love each other.

About forty years later, I begin my day still talking to her. I am with her all day long nearly every day, and I talk her to sleep at night. At that point, she does hang up first.

If you love, you will give time to the one you love.

God knows that. He expects that. If you love Him, you will give Him a lot of your time. Yea, moreover, if you delight in Him, as I delighted in my future wife, you will not be able to keep yourself away from Him, as I could not keep myself away from her.

If you don't love Him, you will naturally avoid Him, and spend your time on that which you do love. If you don't love Him, but think you should, you will try to force yourself to give Him time. Your heart, though, will still go to that which you really desire.

Sabbaths, feasts, sabbath years, Jubilee years—all that time with God—and we didn't even mention the custom of praying three times a day.

David prayed three times a day. We read in Psalms 55:16-17, "As for me, I will call on God. Yahweh will save me. Evening, morning, and at noon, I will cry out in distress. He will hear my voice."

Daniel prayed three times a day, even though he knew it could cost him his life:

> When Daniel knew that the writing was signed, he went into his house (now his windows were open in his chamber toward Jerusalem) and he kneeled on his knees *three times a day*, and prayed, and gave thanks before his God, as he did before. Then these men assembled together, and found Daniel making petition and supplication before his God. Then they came near, and spoke before the king concerning the king's interdict: Haven't you signed an interdict, that every man who shall make petition to any god or man within thirty days, save to you, O king, shall be cast into the den of lions? The king answered, The thing is true, according to the law of the Medes and Persians, which doesn't alter. Then answered they and said before the king, That Daniel, who is of the children of the captivity of Judah, doesn't regard you, O king, nor the interdict that you have signed, but makes his petition *three times a day* (Daniel 6:10-13).

The Temple also had certain hours of prayer, three times a day, which are mentioned in the New Testament. "Peter and John were going up into the temple at the hour of prayer, the ninth hour" (Acts 3:1).

Whew! Yahweh's people, spending all that time with Him, never getting enough, consumed with a love that you cannot suppress—you just can't get enough:

> My eyes stay open through the night watches, that I might meditate on your word (Psalms 119:148).

> God, you are my God. I will earnestly seek you. My soul thirsts for you. My flesh longs for you, in a dry and weary land, where there is no water. So I have seen you in the sanctuary, watching your power and your glory. Because your loving kindness is better than life, my lips shall praise you. So I will bless you while I live. I will lift up my hands in your name. My soul shall be satisfied as with the richest food. My mouth shall praise you with joyful lips, when I remember you on my bed, and think about you in the night watches (Psalms 63:1-6).

> My soul longs for the Lord more than watchmen long for the morning; more than watchmen for the morning (Psalms 130:6).

> My soul longs, and even faints for the courts of Yahweh. My heart and my flesh cry out for the living God (Psalms 84:2).

> As the deer pants for the water brooks, so my soul pants after you, God. My soul thirsts for God, for the living God. When shall I come and appear before God? (Psalms 42:1-2, *World English Bible*).

> I remember the days of old. I meditate on all your doings. I contemplate the work of your hands. I spread forth my hands to you. My soul thirsts for you, like a parched land. Selah (Psalms 143:5-6).

So, then, what do you spend your time on?

How much time do you spend with Yahweh God and Y'shua Messiah each day?

How many times each month do you fast, the way Anna did, just so you can get you out of the way and be closer to your Maker?

How many weeks do you take off each year, for the sole purpose of worshiping God, away from all work and worry?

CHAPTER 11

CHANGING THE SPIRIT

Sabbaths, feasts, sabbath years, Jubilee years, and praying three times a day.

That's the great lesson of the economy that God set up in Israel. If He is your God, and you are His servant, your life can rise above mercenary matters. If you are a spiritual Israelite, you can go beyond the boom-bust cycle. God told Israel they would have enough if they obeyed Him. They could not use that wealth as a basis to get more. They were to use it as a basis to do more with their lives:

> No one can serve two masters, for either he will hate the one and love the other, or he will be devoted to the one and despise the other. You cannot serve God and money. Therefore I tell you, do not be anxious about your life, what you will eat or what you will drink, nor about your body, what you will put on. Is not life more than food, and the body more than clothing? Look at the birds of the air: they neither sow nor reap nor gather into barns, and yet your heavenly Father feeds them. Are you not of more value than they? And which of you by being anxious can add a single hour to his span of life? And why are you anxious about clothing? Consider the lilies of the field, how they grow: they neither toil nor spin, yet I tell you, even Solomon in all his glory was not arrayed like one of these. But if God so clothes the grass of the field, which today is alive and tomorrow is thrown into the oven, will he not much more clothe you, O you of little faith? Therefore do not be anxious, saying, "What shall we eat?" or "What shall we drink?" or "What shall we wear?" For the Gentiles seek

after all these things, and your heavenly Father knows that you need them all. But seek first the kingdom of God and his righteousness, and all these things will be added to you. Therefore do not be anxious about tomorrow, for tomorrow will be anxious for itself. Sufficient for the day is its own trouble (Matthew 6:24-34, ESV).

Is not life more than food, and the body more than clothing?

It is. Humans are spirit beings. No, you can't fly away yet. You're tied to a physical body. But you do have a spirit:

> And Jesus cried out again with a loud voice and yielded up his spirit (Matthew 27:50, ESV).

> And all were weeping and mourning for her, but he said, "Do not weep, for she is not dead but sleeping." And they laughed at him, knowing that she was dead. But taking her by the hand he called, saying, "Child, arise." And her spirit returned, and she got up at once. And he directed that something should be given her to eat (Luke 8:52-55, ESV).

> [T]hese things God has revealed to us through the Spirit. For the Spirit searches everything, even the depths of God. For who knows a person's thoughts except the spirit of that person, which is in him? So also no one comprehends the thoughts of God except the Spirit of God (1 Corinthians 2:10-11, ESV).

You have a spirit, and in that sense, you are a spirit being. No wings, but a lot of potential. Should you, a spirit being tied to a physical body, spend almost all your earthly life on physical things, and mostly ignore the spiritual part?

> How much better it is to get wisdom than gold! Yes, to get understanding is to be chosen rather than silver (Proverbs 16:16).

> Don't weary yourself to be rich. In your wisdom, show restraint. Why do you set your eyes on that which is not? For it certainly sprouts wings like an eagle and flies in the sky (Proverbs 23:4-5).

The lifestyle that God gave to Israel would raise the nation up above the manna and the mundane.

Let's say that you are an Israelite in the wilderness. For years now manna has fallen every day, except for the Sabbath. Every day you know you will have enough, so you never waste your time trying to get too much. You saw the Ten Commandments taught in a sermon at Mount Sinai, when Yahweh Himself came down. The Ten Commandment tablets, written with Yahweh's finger, sit in the Ark of the Covenant in the Tabernacle.

Every day Yahweh's glory was over the Tabernacle. In the daytime it looked like a hovering cloud. When the cloud lifted and moved, Israel took up their camp and followed the cloud. When the cloud stopped, they stopped.

At night when they camped, the presence of God hovered over the Tabernacle like a pillar of fire. God glowed over the whole camp. In the evening you had your meal with your family, *manna au manna*, then relaxed by your tent. You played with your kids, talked with your friends, and always in the background you saw the light from the Tabernacle, the presence of God shining down on you.

Finally, as the evening ebbed, your eyelids looked down at your nose, your heartbeat slowed to a crawl, and it was time for bed. Before you went into your tent to lie down, you looked up. There, in the center of the camp towered the pillar of fire, flickering with a fiery glow, warm, red, and ready to watch over you as you slept.

In the midst of that camp—that incredible camp of Israel— when you woke up every morning, what would you think?

Would you think, *Today I have to get an early start, grab a monut*—that's manna with a hole in it and covered with sugar— *and rush right out and spend all day getting absolutely as much manna as I can get! I've just got to get more manna!*

Would you think that?

I think not. To be in the very presence of God, who gives you the manna, you would focus on God, not the manna.

God is the same today as he was then. Malachi 3:6 says, "I am Yahweh, I change not." That is the choice for each of us in our lives. Will we focus our lives on the manna or on the manna Maker? The follower of Christ today has access to God, just as those Israelites did. He's still just right over there, looking down on us by day and by night.

> We have, then, my friends, *complete freedom to go into the Most Holy Place* by means of the death of Jesus. He opened for us a new way, a living way, through the curtain—that is, through his own body. We have a great priest in charge of the house of God. So *let us come near to God* with a sincere heart and a sure faith, with hearts that have been purified from a guilty conscience and with bodies washed with clean water (Hebrews 10:19-22, GNB).

That is the lesson of the Jubilee cycle. God guarantees you enough. Don't waste your life trying to get more. Spend your life wisely.

What is wise? Having enough time to worship Him, as Israel was to do.

In every Kondratieff Wave, basically the same thing happens. People always get swept up in stuff. They get stuffed with stuff. They have more than enough stuff to live on, but they grow addicted to stuff. They risk all the stuff they have for the chance to get some more stuff.

Meanwhile, in life the real opportunity is to get to know the Creator of the universe. Have you looked at the universe lately? It's a big deal. How about the Creator of all that—is He something or what? Would you like to know Him? He's a spirit being. You're a spirit being. Would you like to have the opportunity to be joined in spirit—mind melded!—with that fantastic spirit being? You have that opportunity:

> I do not cease to give thanks for you, remembering you in my prayers, that the God of our Lord Jesus Christ, the Father of glory, may give you a spirit of wisdom and of revelation in the knowledge of him, having the eyes of your hearts enlightened, that you may know what is the hope to which he has called you, what are the riches of his glorious

inheritance in the saints, and what is the immeasurable greatness of his power toward us who believe, according to the working of his great might that he worked in Chris when he raised him from the dead and seated him at his right hand in the heavenly places, far above all rule and authority and power and dominion, and above every name that is named, not only in this age but also in the one to come (Ephesians 1:16-21, CEV).

So what would you have been like living the Jubilee life?

The Jubilee cycle avoided the aggrandizement of greed and the destruction of indebtedness. What difference would that have made in the life of an individual? If you lived under that system, how would you be at the end of your life?

Fascinating to think about, isn't it? Under that lifestyle, with all that time spent with God, what would you be like at the end of your life?

Look at the normal life today.

Living in America is considered the good life. Most families have at least two vehicles. Most own their own homes, although some now owe more on them than they will sell for. Young people pay as much for a pair of tennis shoes as some foreign workers make in an entire year.

At the same time, they are entangled in the routine panic lifestyle.

What is the routine panic lifestyle?

Almost everybody working almost all the time.

At some time in the distant past, before machines took over, families worked together. It was hard work, plowing, planting, picking—but the family worked together. When industry came along, that took Dad away from the home to work. The world wars took Mom out of the home to work, as most wives do now. And in the most recent generation many teens also work at a job.

Everybody works. Mothers don't have time to be mothers. Kids don't have time to be kids. And Dad works overtime.

It has been calculated that the modern worker spends more time at work than the serfs of the Middle Ages did.

Why does almost everybody work almost all the time?

To get *stuff*.

In the recent boom-bust cycle, were people starving? Did they work so arduously just to stay alive?

No. People work like that to get ahead.

What does *get ahead* mean?

It means to get more.

The routine panic is the constant rush to go there and get here, always pushed for time, always stressed with worry, living life in haste, without taking the time to stop and think about life itself.

What does this routine panic lifestyle do to the people and families who live it?

Families have built bigger and bigger houses, with fancier and more expensive accoutrements, at the same time that those families are being destroyed at a high rate. One of every three American families has been fractured by divorce. Psychologists say that divorce is next to death in trauma. Often divorce does bring death. I have personally known three friends who were brutally dumped by their mates and who died from cancer soon after.

Consider again that amazing statistic. One-third of American families has been destroyed, with terrible trauma for the adults and children. We could not imagine the destruction if a bomb went off that destroyed one-third of American families, yet that is what has happened in an emotional way.

One-half of all marriages now end in divorce. Many have even given up on marriage, and only live together for as long as they can stand each other. Yet about nine out of ten of those couples who just live together will not still be together a decade later. Men and women in such circumstances have no real love, no comfort, no security, and their inevitable children have no family.

But they have *stuff*.

We live in the Missouri Ozarks, once a land of small farms and very friendly people. The topsoil is not deep and the land is not rich, so it is best suited for growing grass and raising animals. Since the end of the Civil War, small farmers either raised milk cows or raised beef cattle. They did not get rich, but it was not a poor life. You could not find friendlier people or better neighbors.

In the last generation, that has changed. Many of the farmers are now part-time farmers. A common farm family will have three jobs. The man works at his job, the woman works at her job, and then they farm as a third job. They have joined the routine panic lifestyle. No longer do they live a relaxed, friendly, small-farm life. They work almost all the time, trying to get ahead.

The family fracture rate here is just as high as anywhere else.

So that's what it's like today. That is normal for now.

What is the goal of this type of life?

To someday be able to retire, and do what you really want to do.

Now if you will think about it, that approach is somewhat illogical. You are admitting that you are spending the bulk of your life doing something you would rather not be doing. You don't really want to work all the time. Finally, when your vigor has vanished, your energy has ebbed, and your health is hobbled— then you are finally going to do what you really want to do.

Between visits to the doctor.

Is that really the wisest course? To spend your whole life doing what you don't want to do, so that at last you can do what you want to do when you're least able to do it?

Again, if you lived the Jubilee lifestyle, the God-given lifestyle, instead of the routine panic lifestyle, how would that have changed you as a person? What would you be like then, at the end of your life?

Remember Moses, the meekest man on earth, who got to spend time hanging out with God? He turned into the Neon Peon:

Yahweh said to Moses, "Chisel two stone tablets like the first: and I will write on the tablets the words that were on the first tablets, which you broke. Be ready by the morning, and come up in the morning to Mount Sinai, and present yourself there to me on the top of the mountain. No one shall come up with you; neither let anyone be seen throughout all the mountain; neither let the flocks nor herds feed before that mountain." He chiseled two tablets of stone like the first; and Moses rose up early in the morning, and went up to Mount Sinai, as Yahweh had commanded him, and took in his hand two stone tablets. Yahweh descended in the cloud, and stood with him there, and proclaimed the name of Yahweh. Yahweh passed by before him, and proclaimed, "Yahweh! Yahweh, a merciful and gracious God, slow to anger, and abundant in loving kindness and truth, keeping loving kindness for thousands, forgiving iniquity and disobedience and sin; and that will by no means clear the guilty, visiting the iniquity of the fathers on the children, and on the children's children, on the third and on the fourth generation." Moses hurried and bowed his head toward the earth, and worshiped (Exodus 34:1-8).

Yahweh said to Moses, "Write you these words: for in accordance with these words I have made a covenant with you and with Israel." He was there with Yahweh forty days and forty nights; he neither ate bread, nor drank water. He wrote on the tablets the words of the covenant, the ten commandments. It happened, when Moses came down from Mount Sinai with the two tablets of the testimony in Moses' hand, when he came down from the mountain, that *Moses didn't know that the skin of his face shone by reason of his speaking with him.* When Aaron and all the children of Israel saw Moses, behold, the skin of his face shone; and they were afraid to come near him. Moses called to them, and Aaron and all the rulers of the congregation returned to him; and Moses spoke to them. Afterward all the children of Israel came near, and he gave them all of the commandments that Yahweh had spoken with him on Mount Sinai. When Moses was done speaking with them, he put a veil on his face. But when Moses went in before Yahweh to speak with him, he took the veil off, until he came out; and he came out, and spoke to the children of Israel that which he was commanded. The children of Israel

> saw Moses' face, that the skin of Moses' face shone: and Moses put the veil on his face again, until he went in to speak with him (Exodus 34:27-35).

Why did Moses' face shine? Because he had spent time with Yahweh. Moses had the God glow.

If you spend time with God, it is absolutely inevitable that your life, your person, your spirit will be changed. You will get the God glow.

If you lived the Jubilee lifestyle, the God-given lifestyle, how would that change you as a person? What would you be like then, at the end of your life?

Each Sabbath day is spent not working, not playing, not even thinking about such ordinary things, but delighting in spiritual contact with the Great Spirit, the giver of life.

Three times a year you feast on God, rehearsing His plan for all humankind. Your work world is left far behind for the spiritual world. Food, fellowship, and faith fill these festivals, three times a year, every year.

Every sabbath year you take off from your work for a whole year. What will you do during that year? What is it that your heart most yearns after?

Since you wouldn't be planting or reaping that year, perhaps you could do a little work to make some more money on the side. You know, try to work a little extra to get ahead. That way, the year wouldn't be a total waste.

Or since God had guaranteed you enough anyway, what if you spent that whole year just trying to serve Him? Using that whole year for extra study, meditation, and communication with the one your spirit most yearns after. And using time to help others, in any way that they might need help.

Wouldn't it be wonderful to spend a whole year just serving God and others?

If you actually spent a year doing that, would you be the same person at the end of that year?

If, in a half century, you spent seven whole sabbath years just serving God and others, how would that shape you as a person?

Then, in the Jubilee year of your lifetime, the second year in a row that you would be off from normal work, you could reflect deeply on your life—where you had been, and where you are going. The end of your life would just be the beginning.

If you spent that much time in your life getting God instead of seeking stuff, what would you be like when you were seventy years old and ready to move on to the next level? Only God knows what He could do with you, if you give Him the time. But I absolutely know one thing—after seventy years of such a life, you would have the God glow.

When your Jubilee cycle is complete, and you come to the end of your life, what is it that you will want to have then, an IRA or an ERA—Eternal Retirement Account?

The great lesson of this Jubilee life is that you don't focus on this life. This life is not the destination. It's just the journey. This life is not the program. It's just the boot. This life is not life. It always ends in death. The real life—the life that does not end in death—is yet to come.

Isaiah said:

> The Spirit of the Lord Yahweh is on me; because Yahweh has anointed me to preach good news to the humble. He has sent me to bind up the brokenhearted, to proclaim liberty to the captives, and release to those who are bound; to proclaim the year of Yahweh's favor, and the day of vengeance of our God; to comfort all who mourn (Isaiah 61:1-2).

This is referring to the Jubilee year: *to proclaim liberty to the captives, and release those who are bound, to proclaim the year of Yahweh's favor.* Christ began his teaching by referring to that scripture about the Jubilee:

> And Jesus returned in the power of the Spirit to Galilee, and a report about him went out through all the surrounding country. And he taught in their synagogues, being glorified

by all. And he came to Nazareth, where he had been brought up. And as was his custom, he went to the synagogue on the Sabbath day, and he stood up to read. And the scroll of the prophet Isaiah was given to him. He unrolled the scroll and found the place where it was written, "The Spirit of the Lord is upon me, because he has anointed me to proclaim good news to the poor. He has sent me to proclaim liberty to the captives and recovering of sight to the blind, to set at liberty those who are oppressed, to proclaim the year of the Lord's favor." And he rolled up the scroll and gave it back to the attendant and sat down. And the eyes of all in the synagogue were fixed on him. And he began to say to them, "Today this Scripture has been fulfilled in your hearing" (Luke 4:14-21, ESV).

The Messiah began His teaching with the Jubilee year, because that was the beginning of granting liberty to the captives and oppressed.

Why does the Kondratieff Wave exist? If people can read about it, and know that there is a cycle which can be traced back to the 1200s, why don't they take pains to avoid the boom-bust cycle?

The long wave exists because people are captives of their selfish nature:

We know that the Law is spiritual; but I am a mortal, sold as a slave to sin. I do not understand what I do; for I don't do what I would like to do, but instead I do what I hate. Since what I do is what I don't want to do, this shows that I agree that the Law is right. So I am not really the one who does this thing; rather it is the sin that lives in me. I know that good does not live in me—that is, in my human nature. For even though the desire to do good is in me, I am not able to do it. I don't do the good I want to do; instead, I do the evil that I do not want to do. If I do what I don't want to do, this means that I am no longer the one who does it; instead, it is the sin that lives in me. So I find that this law is at work: when I want to do what is good, what is evil is the only choice I have. My inner being delights in the law of God. But I see a different law at work in my body—a law that fights against the law which my mind approves of. It makes me a prisoner to the law of sin which is at work in my body. What an unhappy man I

am! Who will rescue me from this body that is taking me
to death? (Romans 7:14-24, GNB).

Paul said that we are sold as a slave to sin. Just as an indebted
Hebrew was sold as a slave to pay his debts, and usually could
not escape that debt or enslavement on his own, so humans
are sold into slavery to their own natures, from which they do
not have the power to escape.

Humans cannot stop the long wave. Each time they say,
"This time it's different." And each time it's the same.

Humans cannot stop war. They talk peace, and they hate
war, but they cannot avoid it. The farther man's technology
and knowledge advances, the more brutal his wars become.
The Age of Reason or the Age of Enlightenment brought an
emphasis on reason and education as the solution to man's
perpetual problems, and a rejection of God's revelation. Since
that time of human enlightenment, wars have become even
worse. Mankind uses his education ultimately not to refine his
nature, but to refine his killing capacity.

In the Jubilee year, people were returned to their first
estate; slaves were set free; and prisoners were released.

Humans have lost their first estate. Their first property
was Eden, without sin and with direct contact with Yahweh
God Himself. From that time, we have been enslaved by a
nature that is at enmity with God, imprisoned by a mountain
of debt that we can never repay.

But—thank God—there is the Jubilee.

When that last trumpet sounds, because of our redeemer,
our near kinsman, we will return to our first estate, our
original family property...*living next door to God*:

> Soon after the trouble of those days, the sun will grow
> dark, the moon will no longer shine, the stars will fall
> from heaven, and the powers in space will be driven from
> their courses. Then the sign of the Son of Man will appear
> in the sky; and all the peoples of earth will weep as they
> see the Son of Man coming on the clouds of heaven with

power and great glory. The great trumpet will sound, and he will send out his angels to the four corners of the earth, and they will gather his chosen people from one end of the world to the other (Matthew 24:29-31, GNB).

Just as we wear the likeness of the man made of earth, so we will wear the likeness of the Man from heaven. What I mean, friends, is that what is made of flesh and blood cannot share in God's Kingdom, and what is mortal cannot possess immortality. Listen to this secret truth: we shall not all die, but when the last trumpet sounds, we shall all be changed in an instant, as quickly as the blinking of an eye. For when the trumpet sounds, the dead will be raised, never to die again, and we shall all be changed (1 Corinthians 15:49-51, GNB).

There will be the shout of command, the archangel's voice, the sound of God's trumpet, and the Lord himself will come down from heaven. Those who have died believing in Christ will rise to life first; then we who are living at that time will be gathered up along with them in the clouds to meet the Lord in the air. And so we will always be with the Lord. So then, encourage one another with these words (1 Thessalonians 4:16-18, GNB).

Then the seventh angel blew his trumpet, and there were loud voices in heaven, saying, "The power to rule over the world belongs now to our Lord and his Messiah, and he will rule forever and ever!" (Revelations 11:15, GNB).

Jubilation!

What happens at the end of the age of man is the very last boom-bust cycle. That will be an economic boom greater than any before it. Truly, nearly everyone on earth will think, "This time it's different."

But it won't be. At the end-time Jubilee, the greatest economic prosperity the world has ever known—truly worldwide under a worldwide power—will fall in the greatest bear market ever imagined:

After this I saw another angel coming down out of heaven. He had great authority, and his splendor brightened the whole earth. He cried out in a loud voice:

"She has fallen! Great Babylon has fallen! She is now
haunted by demons and unclean spirits; all kinds of filthy
and hateful birds live in her. For all the nations have
drunk her wine—the strong wine of her immoral lust. The
kings of the earth practiced sexual immorality with her,
and the merchants of the world grew rich from her
unrestrained lust." Then I heard another voice from
heaven, saying, "Come out, my people! Come out from
her! You must not take part in her sins; you must not share
in her punishment! For her sins are piled up as high as
heaven, and God remembers her wicked ways"
(Revelations 18:1-5, GNB).

Notice that this is a description of a worldwide economic
union that will be enormously successful in spreading the
wealth around. Christ says that all nations have drunk of her
wine. The merchants of the earth grew rich from her
unrestrained lust. Yet God's people are not a part of this.

"Come out, my people! Come out from her!"

Does that surprise you?

This worldwide economic empire will have brought
capitalistic prosperity to the whole world. Even the third
world countries will be part of this, those emerging nations
that have so long languished in poverty and deprivation. All
nations of the earth will be prosperous beyond anything they
have ever known. And they will love it!

But God's people will not be a part of that rich system.

"Come out, my people! Come out from her!"

You see, the great choice in life is either God or gold. Each
one demands all your life. You cannot serve God and mammon.
Christ said that. Do you believe it?

You cannot serve both God and mammon. You must either
be a Mammonite or an Israelite. Those Israelites who did not
give Yahweh His time were not true Israelites. When they quit
giving Him their time, they weren't His anymore.

If you think that you *can* serve both God and mammon,
you are already a Mammonite. Your heart has been won by
the god of gold, and you do not want to give up that treasure.

Again, God's people will not be part of this great end-time economic boom. They will be storing up riches of another kind. And they will avoid the mother of all bear markets;

> Treat her exactly as she has treated you; pay her back double for all she has done. Fill her cup with a drink twice as strong as the drink she prepared for you. Give her as much suffering and grief as the glory and luxury she gave herself. For she keeps telling herself: "Here I sit, a queen! I am no widow, I will never know grief!" Because of this, in one day she will be struck with plagues—disease, grief, and famine. And she will be burned with fire, because the Lord God, who judges her, is mighty (Revelations 18:6-8, GNB).

Notice the great emphasis on wealth for the end-time power:

> The kings of the earth who took part in her immorality and lust will cry and weep over the city when they see the smoke from the flames that consume her. They stand a long way off, because they are afraid of sharing in her suffering. They say, "How terrible! How awful! This great and mighty city Babylon! In just one hour you have been punished!" The *merchants* of the earth also cry and mourn for her, because no one *buys* their goods any longer; no one *buys* their gold, silver, precious stones, and pearls; their goods of linen, purple cloth, silk, and scarlet cloth; all kinds of rare woods and all kinds of objects made of ivory and of expensive wood, of bronze, iron, and marble; and cinnamon, spice, incense, myrrh, and frankincense; wine and oil, flour and wheat, cattle and sheep, horses and carriages, slaves, and even human lives (Revelations 18:9-13, GNB).

Look at all that stuff! Nearly all of mankind, living in the lap of luxury! This economy is not need-based. It is greed–based:

> The merchants say to her, "All the good things you longed to own have disappeared, and all your *wealth and glamor* are gone, and you will never find them again!" The merchants, who became *rich* from doing business in that city, will stand a long way off, because they are afraid of sharing in her suffering. They will cry and mourn, and say, "How terrible! How awful for the great city! She used

> to dress herself in linen, purple, and scarlet, and cover herself with gold ornaments, precious stones, and pearls! And *in one hour she has lost all this wealth!*" (Revelations 18:14-17a, GNB).

Bear market! Dow Jones down 100,000 points today!

> All the ships' captains and passengers, the sailors and all others who earn their living on the sea, stood a long way off, and cried out as they saw the smoke from the flames that consumed her: "There never has been another city like this great city!" They threw dust on their heads, they cried and mourned, saying, "How terrible! How awful for the great city! She is the city where all who have ships sailing the seas became rich on her wealth! And in one hour she has lost everything!" (Revelations 18:17b-19, GNB).

Notice the different reactions here. Those whose riches are in stuff are sad. Those whose riches are in God are glad:

> Be glad, heaven, because of her destruction! Be glad, God's people and the apostles and prophets! For God has condemned her for what she did to you! Then a mighty angel picked up a stone the size of a large millstone and threw it into the sea, saying, "This is how the great city Babylon will be violently thrown down and will never be seen again. The music of harps and of human voices, of players of the flute and the trumpet, will never be heard in you again! No workman in any trade will ever be found in you again; and the sound of the millstone will be heard no more! Never again will the light of a lamp be seen in you; no more will the voices of brides and grooms be heard in you. Your merchants were the most powerful in all the world, and with your false magic you deceived all the peoples of the world!" Babylon was punished because the blood of prophets and of God's people was found in the city; yes, the blood of all those who have been killed on earth (Revelations 18:20-24, GNB).

The result of this rich empire is evil. The object of that evil is those people who will not participate in the system, who will not be a part of her unity, which was a whole way of life— riches and religion.

Ultimately, the desire for riches *is* a religion.

In the Jubilee system, someone who had sold his land or his freedom could be redeemed by a relative. In the Book of Ruth, her husband had died. She was redeemed by a relative, Boaz, who redeemed her husband's land and his widow, Ruth. Boaz then took her as his bride.

At the end, Christ redeems those who are in His family, and takes them as His bride:

> After this I heard what seemed to be the loud voice of a great multitude in heaven, crying out, "Hallelujah! Salvation and glory and power belong to our God, for his judgments are true and just; for he has judged the great prostitute who corrupted the earth with her immorality, and has avenged on her the blood of his servants." Once more they cried out, "Hallelujah! The smoke from her goes up forever and ever." And the twenty-four elders and the four living creatures fell down and worshiped God who was seated on the throne, saying, "Amen. Hallelujah!" And from the throne came a voice saying, "Praise our God, all you his servants, you who fear him, small and great." Then I heard what seemed to be the voice of a great multitude, like the roar of many waters and like the sound of mighty peals of thunder, crying out, "Hallelujah! For the Lord our God the Almighty reigns. Let us rejoice and exult and give him the glory, for the marriage of the Lamb has come, and his Bride has made herself ready" (Revelations 19:1-7, ESV).

Finally, the human race is brought back to its first estate, the original property, living next door to God:

> Then I saw a new heaven and a new earth, for the first heaven and the first earth had passed away, and the sea was no more. And I saw the holy city, new Jerusalem, coming down out of heaven from God, prepared as a bride adorned for her husband. And I heard a loud voice from the throne saying, "Behold, the dwelling place of God is with man. He will dwell with them, and they will be his people, and God himself will be with them as their God" (Revelations 21:1-3, ESV).

That will be the end of the boom-bust cycle. That cycle exists in human history because of human nature. The lesson of that cycle is to focus on that which overcomes your human nature. God set the Jubilee system up to give His people enough physically so they could live spiritually.

Each one of us has that choice today.

We do not live in a system where we are given a parcel of land, debt-free. We do pay taxes to human governments. Our loans are not canceled every seven years. In most jobs, if we try to take off the seventh year, we will almost certainly be cast off from that job in the eighth year, too. What can we do?

How much we can do is determined by how much we love God.

Cain asked the question, "Am I my brother's keeper?"

The Kondratieff Wave is caused by built-up excess from people giving the wrong answer to that question. Christ answered that question correctly:

> For while we were still weak, at the right time Christ died for the ungodly. For one will scarcely die for a righteous person—though perhaps for a good person one would dare even to die—but God shows his love for us in that while we were still sinners, Christ died for us (Romans 5:6-8, ESV).

The Godly died for the ungodly. The Creator gave up Himself for His creation. He who was being killed prayed for His killers—Jews and Gentiles—while they were killing Him.

He was contra-Cain. The sinless One died for the sinner before the sinner had even repented. That is *really* being your brother's keeper.

I am the ungodly one He died for. I am the creation He gave Himself for. I am the killer He prayed for. I am Barabbas, the murderer freed at Passover.

After all that, and after all that He has given me, the question of my life is, *how much will I give to God and others?* How much will I serve myself? How much will I serve Him?

God has guaranteed to supply all our needs through His riches in Christ Jesus. If God expected an Israelite to spend much of his life with Him, then He expects at least as much from Christians. Our purpose in life is just as high as theirs: to love God with all our hearts and to love our neighbors as ourselves.

God guaranteed Israel that if they obeyed Him, they would have enough. They would be taken care of. Therefore, they could focus their lives not on getting, but on giving.

Dedicated followers of Christ have the same guarantee today. We will be taken care of. Therefore, we can center our lives around God and Christ. And we so eagerly look forward to that day of the great Jubilee, when we will be fully restored to our property, and live right next to God.

CHAPTER 1: NIKOLAI AND MOSES

1. Nikolai Kondratieff, *The Long Waves in Economic Life* (New York: Knopf: Distributed by Random House, 1991), originally published in Russia, 1935.

2. George Modelski, "Kondratieff (or K-) Waves," University of Washington Faculty, online at https://faculty.washington.edu/modelski/IPEKWAVE.html (accessed 4/30/09).

3. Ibid.

4. New World Encyclopedia contributors, "Nikolai Kondratiev," *New World Encyclopedia*, online at http://www.newworldencyclopedia.org/entry/Nikolai_Kondratiev?oldid=686639 (accessed 5/3/09).

5. J. J. van Duijn, *The Long Wave in Economic Life* (London: Allen & Unwin, 1983), a synopsis of the book is at "Economy Professor: A Dictionary of Economic Terms, Concepts, Theories & Theorists" "Kondratieff Cycles," online at http://www.economyprofessor.com/economictheories/kondratieff-cycles.php (accessed 5/1/09).

6. Dr. Joseph de Beauchamp, financial advisor and CEO/President of World Financial News Network, Publisher of Financial Information, "How does the Economic Theory contribute to managerial decisions?" October 9, 2006, online at http://en.allexperts.com/q/Economics-2301/Economic-Theory.htm#b (accessed 4/30/09).

7. Joseph Farah, "Forgive Us Our Debts," WorldNetDaily.com, October 13, 2008, online at http://www.worldnetdaily.com/index.php?fa=PAGE.view&pageId=77656 (accessed 4/30/09).

8. David Chapman, "Technical Scoop, Kondratieff Wave Cycles," Gold-Eagle.com, June 29, 2002, online at http://gold-eagle.com/editorials_02/chapmand062902.html (accessed 5/3/09).

9. Jon Hilsenrath, Serena Ng, and Damian Paletta, "Worst Crisis Since '30s, With No End In Sight," Wall Street Journal Digital Network, September 18, 2008, online at http://online.wsj.com/article/SB122169431617549947.html (accessed 4/30/09).

10. Ibid.

11. Henry Paulson, former Treasury secretary under President George W. Bush, in a White House press briefing, September 15, 2008, online at http://georgewbush-whitehouse.archives.gov/news/releases/2008/09/20080915-8.html (accessed 4/30/09).

12. Ibid.

13. Laura Rowley, "The Financial Crisis: Getting to the Roots," YahooFinance.com, September 17, 2008, online at http://finance.yahoo.com/expert/article/moneyhappy/108581 (accessed 4/30/09).

14. Alan Greenspan, "Greenspan: Tough decisions await in Lehman case," Associated Press, FoxNews.com, September 14, 2008, analysis of an interview of the former Fed chairman on *This Week* on ABC, online at http://www.foxnews.com/wires/2008Sep14/0,4670,Greenspan,00.html (accessed 5/1/09).

15. Ellis W. Tallman and Jon R. Moen, "Lessons from the Panic of 1907," *Economic Review*, May/June 1990, 1, 3, online at http://fraser.stlouisfed.org/docs/meltzer/talles90.pdf (accessed 4/30/09).

16. *Second Thoughts: Myths and Morals of U.S. Economic History*, a collection of essays edited by Donald N. McCloskey, Chapter 12, "The Great Depression, Can It Happen Again," John Wallis, 96-97.

17. Laura Ingalls Wilder, *On the Way Home* (New York: Harper and Row, 1962), 65.

18. "Houses Getting Bigger: It's Official: The Government Reports That Houses Have Grown in Size Over the Past 30 Years," American Moving & Storage Association, online at http://promover.org/PR_NewsRoom/Direction/Aug%2006/8-06HousesBigger.pdf; Steve W. Rawlings, "Households and Families," U.S. Census Bureau, graph "Households by Size: 1970-1994," online at http://www.census.gov/population/www/pop-profile/hhfam.html (accessed 4/30/09).

CHAPTER 2 : NATURAL LAW

1. John Robbins, *Healthy at 100: The Scientifically Proven Secrets of the World's Healthiest and Longest-Lived Peoples* (New York: Random House), 2006, "Love and Healthcare," 218.

CHAPTER 4 : MANNA AND MONEY

1. Adam Smith, *An Inquiry into the Nature and Causes of the Wealth of Nations*, ed. Edwin Cannan (Chicago: University of Chicago Press; Facsimile of 1904 edition, February 15, 1977), Book IV, Chapter 2, "Of Restraints upon the Importation from Foreign Countries of such Goods as can be Produced at Home," 477-478.

CHAPTER 6 : LIVING THE GOOD LIFE: THE SABBATH

1. William McEwen, Xiaoguang Fang, Chuanping Zhang, and Richard Burkholder, "Inside the Mind of the Chinese Consumer," *Harvard Business Review*, March 2006, 4, online at http://custom.hbsp.com/custom/ GALLUR0603D2006030653.pdf, accessed 5/1/09.

2. Kristen Fischer, "How to Know if a Job is Making You Sick," Ehow.com, available online at http://www.ehow.com/how_2049840_ know-job-making-sick.html, accessed 5/1/09.

CHAPTER 9 : THE JUBILEE

1. James Orr, ed., "Jubilee Year," *International Standard Bible Encyclopedia*, vol. 3, (Chicago: The Howard-Severance Company, 1915).

CHAPTER 10 : THE WHOLE JUBILEE SYSTEM

1. Joseph Farah, "Forgive Us Our Debts," WorldNetDaily.com, October 13, 2008, online at http://www.worldnetdaily.com/index.php?fa= PAGE.view&pageId=77656 (accessed 4/30/09)

2. Jeannine Aversa, "Stress Over Debt Taking Toll on Health," *USA Today*, June 6, 2008, online at http://www.usatoday.com/news/health/ 2008-06-09-debt-stress_N.htm, accessed 5/1/09.

3. John P. Foley, ed., Notation 2017, "Debt, Tormented by," The Jeffersonian Cyclopedia, (New York and London: Funk & Wagnalls Company, 1900), 230. Also see Independent (London), "US Presidents' Lives," "Thomas Jefferson," January 17, 2009, online at http://www.independent.co.uk/news/presidents/ thomas-jefferson-1391129.html, accessed 5/1/09.

4. Kristin Graham and Alyce Lomax, "The Death of Excessive Luxury," Motley Fool, November 10, 2008, online at http://www.fool.com/investing/ general/2008/11/10/the-death-of-excessive-luxury.aspx, accessed 5/3/09.

Made in the USA